THE AUTHOR: Jōzan Hirota was born in 1896 in Itoigawa City, Niigata Prefecture. He began studying Bonkei in 1917. In 1936 he founded and became headmaster of the Nunagawa School of Bonkei. In 1948 he obtained the cooperation of other schools of Bonkei in reestablishing the Japan Bonkei Association. He is currently the Association's Executive Director. Among his principal works on Bonkei are *Bankei to Bonkei* ("Bankei and Bonkei") and *Shumi no Bonkei* ("Bonkei as a Hobby").

THE MASTERS' BOOK OF BONSAI
By the Directors of the Japan Bonsai Association

This beautiful work gives a comprehensive explanation of the art of growing miniature trees. It contains 140 pages, $8\frac{1}{2} \times 8$ inches; 24 full color photos, 100 black-and-white, boxed.
$5.95

SAIKEI: Living Landscapes in Miniature
By Toshio Kawamoto

This unique volume reveals the techniques used in making tiny gardens with living trees. 133 pages, $10\frac{1}{2} \times 7\frac{1}{2}$ inches, boxed, 21 color pages, 350 black-and-white, 50 line drawings.
$6.95

Bonkei

盆景

Bonkei: TRAY LANDSCAPES

By JŌZAN HIROTA

Photographs by YOSHIKAZU EZAKI

講 談 社

KODANSHA   INTERNATIONAL   LTD : Tokyo, Japan & Palo Alto, Calif., U.S.A.

DISTRIBUTORS:
British Commonwealth (excluding Canada)
WARD LOCK & COMPANY LTD.
London and Melbourne

Continental Europe
BOXERBOOKS, INC.
Zurich

The Far East
JAPAN PUBLICATIONS TRADING CO.
C.P.O. Box 722, Tokyo

Published by KODANSHA INTERNATIONAL LTD.,
2-12-21, Otowa, Bunkyo-ku, Tokyo, Japan and KODAN-
SHA INTERNATIONAL/USA, LTD., 577 College
Avenue, Palo Alto, California 94306. Copyright © 1970
by Kodansha International Ltd. All rights reserved.
Library of Congress Catalog Card No. 79-117384
S.B.N. 87011-124-8; J.B.C. 2076-781437-2361
First edition, 1970

745.92
H66b

TABLE OF CONTENTS

EXAMPLES OF FINISHED BONKEI

A Village in the Mountains ▷
The focal point of this bonkei is the house
and Japanese white cedar on the right. The
season is autumn, after the rice harvest.
Pampas grass, the red persimmon tree, and
the artificial yellow moss sprinkled on the
mountains all indicate the time of year. The
thatched house, built by the artist himself,
is typical of the mountainous regions of
Japan.

A WATERWHEEL BESIDE
A FARMHOUSE
This bonkei, by the strategic
placing of the foreground,
middle, and distant areas, pos-
sesses an internal movement.
The eye is led from the bushes
in the left foreground along
the stream to the bamboo
field, represented by reeds,
then on from the house up to
the artificial pine that stands
beside the stark tree trunk.

KYOTO'S GINKAKUJI TEMPLE

Centrally placed, the temple links the ornamental pond of white wave sand in the left foreground to the water on the right, represented by blue sand. The living plants used are Japanese white cedars on the left, and field grass and moss in the temple garden. An artificial pine stands in front of the temple.

12

◁A River in a Mountain Gorge
The figure poling his raft down the
swift current that divides the foreground from the village and its massive surroundings in the distance gives
a sense of motion to this bonkei.
Clumps of saxifrage occupy the centre
foreground, and living moss represents
forests on the summit at the rear of
the tray. A wooden suspension bridge
and baskets for collecting stones at the
river's edge provide added interest.

A House by a Lake
This is a placid scene. To the right of
the house, Japanese white cedars have
been planted, while a tall spruce rises
to the left of the scene. Artificial
cypress trees behind the house lend a
sense of distance to the landscape.
Flowering artificial cherry trees indicate that the season is spring.

13

◁ THE INLAND SEA IN AUTUMN

Here a late autumn is expressed by the deepening yellow of the bushes, the foaming breakers, and two ships making for shelter. A living pine grows to the right of the rocks, and two artificial pines stand out against the distant skyline. Living moss in the right foreground

MATSUSHIMA—A BEAUTY SPOT IN JAPAN

Small islands, made of *keto* (peat), are scattered about the tray. Harmony is brought to this bonkei, though, by the line of ships that links the large island on the left to the smaller ones in the right background. Each island is planted with living moss and artificial pine trees.

MIST IN DEEP MOUNTAINS
The summits of these steep mountains are bare. To emphasize their steepness, the artist has used white clay in greater quantity than on other more gentle inclines, and the foothills are sprinkled with green and yellow mosses up to the limit of the flower zone. White mist, made of thin strips of cotton wool, floats among the rocks. By placing a clump of living trees and bare tree trunks on the right, a balance is maintained with the mountain range on the left of the tray.

MT. FUJI BY THE LAKESIDE

This mountain's basic shape lends itself ideally to the needs of the beginner. Mt. Fuji is also a useful indication of the prevailing season, being half-covered by snow in spring and autumn, snowbound in winter, and only topped with snow in summer. Here, its melting snows are echoed in the early blooms of spring that surround the house. Living moss denotes a distant forest on the lower slopes of Fuji.

◁ MOUNTAIN AND MARSHLAND
A mountain with two thatched houses takes up the middle distant scene. Tall reeds and cardamine are in the right foreground, while stagnant water, suggested by sand dyed a deep blue and fringed by moss, occupies the centre foreground. Japanese white cedars lie behind the reeds, and a small pine branch breaks the outline of the left side of the mountain.

THE MOUNTAINS OF NIKKO
This bonkei combines three themes: a shrine, Nikko's Kegon waterfall, and the mountains in which it has its source. The composition leads one from the Japanese andromeda tree in the left foreground across the bridge to the shrine, around which assorted cypresses and artificial cedars have been planted. This movement continues from the shrine up the mountain ridge to the summit. Below, the white fall of water stands out in vivid contrast to the dark rock.

A CASTLE BY THE SEA

A needle juniper tree occupies the right foreground, and the castle, constructed by the artist himself, stands in the middle distance. Green artificial moss has been added as a final touch to complete the realism of the rocks. The white crests of the waves, and the two ships, give a sense of motion to this otherwise peaceful scene.

This framed bonkei, intended to be hung on a wall, is composed of the same type of material as that used in a dry bonkei; the sky is made out of sand and adhesive. Many are attracted by the three-dimensionality of framed bonkei, which permits a greater realism than might be attained by oil painting.

The basic material of this dry bonkei is papier-mâché mixed with clay. Its advantage over *keto* is that it lasts for a much longer period of time. Plants, trees, and flowers used in a dry bonkei are all artificial.

Here, the artist has chosen to represent a Chinese landscape, set in the T'ang era. Two figures can be seen between the five-storied pagoda in the right foreground and the castle gate; beyond is the castle itself and, higher still, a temple below the mountain's summit.

There is no reason why bonkei should be confined to Japanese themes. This *keto* bonkei, using real flowers and trees as well as artificial ones, depicts an early American scene. Transparent nylon or plastic give an effective impression of a fountain's jet of water.

Chapter 1 BONKEI AND ITS BACKGROUND

Perhaps the simplest way to introduce bonkei to the foreigner who is unfamiliar with it is to define the Japanese characters of which the word is composed: *bon* (meaning a tray or any other similarly shallow container), and *kei* (which derives from *keshiki*, a "landscape"). Thus, bonkei is a miniature landscape within the confines of a smallish, shallow tray (usually eighteen by six inches and seldom more than an inch deep), which may be placed anywhere in the house. It is as portable as a painting or a small piece of sculpture. In the Japanese household, it is usually to be found in the *tokonoma*, the alcove where the family displays certain of its valued objects from time to time. But there is no reason, obviously, why a bonkei should not be displayed anywhere.

It has another feature in common with landscape painting, namely that nature is seen through the creator's eyes. Both, then, are personal and harmonious reconstructions of what the creator has seen. Just as no two people will view the same scene with the same eyes, so the bonkei they create of that scene will have different points of emphasis. Suppose, for example, that two people are looking at a rocky landscape above a rough sea. One may be impressed chiefly by the huge waves breaking against the cliffs, while the other is more deeply moved by the towering cliffs themselves, or by frail sailing boats making their uncertain way through the waves. Obviously, when they both create their bonkei, these differences in outlook will be reflected in their work. Thus bonkei can be as interesting, as individual, and as communicative as painting itself. One important difference is that bonkei, unlike painting, makes use of a relatively small range of colors; its chief beauty, therefore, derives from harmony of form and shape—for bonkei is, of course, three-dimensional. It may be thought of, in a sense, as a combination of landscape painting and sculpture—yet it has the advantage of being a far easier art for the amateur to master.

All the technical knowledge required is given in this book, as are the materials used, which may be as few or as many as one chooses. The one indispensable possession is an eye for the beauty in nature; for bonkei, while it miniaturizes the world, seeks to idealize it too. In Japan, particularly, bonkei concentrates on the beauty of the changing seasons, which, to the Japanese, has always been one of the most fascinating aspects of their kaleidoscopic country.

Bonkei is thought to be one of Japan's oldest arts, dating back to the reign of the empress Suiko (A.D. 554–628), who was presented with an incense stand by the imperial court of China, and who conceived the idea of filling the base with sand and placing in the sand a harmonious arrangement of small stones. Legend also has it that during the reign of the same empress a naturalized Korean created a miniature of Mount Shumi in the South Garden of the Imperial Palace. (Shumi, according to Buddhist tradition, is held to be the center of the world, a sacred mountain where Buddhist saints live in eternal youth.) Other Koreans who had been shipwrecked in Japan are also said to have created a miniature of Shumi to the west of Asuka Temple. Presumably, then, it was a custom to recreate the sacred mountain in miniature, and this may well have been the origin of bonkei; in any case, very little is known about this early period.

Yoshimasa, the eighth Ashikaga shogun (1435–90), who encouraged both *ikebana* and the tea ceremony, is also said to have been instrumental in popularizing bonkei, but it was not until late in the nineteenth century that a bonkei master, Chisen Izumi, discovered how to mold *keto* with a spatula to create mountains, rocks, and fields: a crucial and dramatic moment in the history of bonkei.

Keto is a kind of peat; generally, the vegetable matter of

An illustration from the "Kasuga Gongen" scroll made in the beginning of the 14th century.

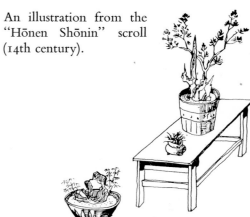

An illustration from the "Hōnen Shōnin" scroll (14th century).

24

which it is composed has grown in or near marshland and after dying has lain in the soil for a long time. *Keto* is first dried, when it is light brown, and then, after being mixed with water and kneaded, becomes as malleable as light clay, and dark in color. It is invaluable to present-day bonkei.

In fact, its discovery gave rise to a number of schools, all of which use it. Some also use rocks and stones as well as grass and moss. My own school, the Nunagawa, uses trees, grass, and moss in addition to the *keto* out of which mountains and rocks are formed. This school is named after Princess Nunagawa, consort of Ōkuninushi no Mikoto, an ancient deity, who is said to have been born in Nunagawa, present-day Itoigawa, in Niigata Prefecture.

My school invariably makes use of living flora, for we feel that only in this way can the true beauty of nature be expressed, and we also use, as do some other schools, miniature houses, boats, and the like, as well as human and animal figures. Furthermore, we emphasize the importance of harmony in seasonal representations by placing trees with broad leaves, for example, in the foreground, while those with smaller leaves are arranged in the background. We insist that our scenes follow a natural rhythm, in the belief that anything that is false to nature is alien to bonkei. Thus, particular attention is paid to a close observation of nature, never forgetting at the same time that the final work, however faithful to the original scene, must be personal and individual.

Bonkei, incidentally, is not the only art form in Japan that specializes in the reproduction of natural scenes in miniature. There is also *bonseki*, where stones play the major role; *bonsai*, which makes chief use of plants; and *bankei*, where *keto* is the primary material.

Any of these may be used in Japan on such formal occasions as weddings and funerals. A marriage ceremony, for example, might feature a bonkei decorated with pine trees and figures of the Old Man and Old Woman—symbols in Japan of longevity and marital happiness—while a bonkei made for a funeral might be composed of plants for which the deceased had had a special liking. There are any number of Buddhist rituals for which special bonkei might be created, as well as for ordinary gatherings, where the bonkei becomes a special display piece. Similarly, a carefully composed bonkei may be placed in a guest's room as a token of homage and welcome.

Ikebana is of course used in the same way, but whereas flowers have but a transitory beauty, a bonkei, if properly watered, may last a long time. When dry bonkei methods are adopted, then the life of the work may be prolonged still further. As with a flower arrangement, a bonkei may be moved from place to place, and with each removal it appears fresh and new and gives added luster to its surroundings.

Bonkei recreates, in the tray in which it is arranged, miniature landscapes that may be based on such themes as fields and mountains, valleys, fantastically shaped rocks, rivers and waterfalls, the sea and the shore—or a combination of any or all of them. Thus, it makes a special appeal to those who appreciate the unspoiled beauties of nature. Those most keenly sensitive to trees and plants will probably find my own school of bonkei arrangement most satisfactory. Bonkei prefers a dramatic composition and so affords one the only means by which a grandiose natural scene may be taken into the house and kept there for constant aesthetic pleasure. Bonkei recreates and communicates the beauty that is inherent in natural harmony.

I cannot stress too strongly the importance of the element of harmony in bonkei; without it, the resulting work is discordant and can move neither the creator himself nor the viewer. Suppose, for example, you wish to make a seascape with pine trees growing along the shore: you cannot possibly achieve the necessary harmony until you have first determined how many trees to include in the finished work and where they should be placed. If your evaluation is incorrect, the viewer of the completed bonkei will only feel dissatisfied; he will know that something is wrong, though he may not know exactly what the error is.

There are three ancient conditions (*Sansui no Sanpō*) that apply to Eastern painting; they apply equally well to bonkei. According to these ancient rules, the completed landscape, whether two- or three-dimensional, must look (1) deep and distant, (2) tall and distant, and (3) wide and distant. Perhaps

Suiban Bonkei

a mountainous country like Japan, with its deep gorges and swift-flowing rivers, lends itself more easily to the application of these ancient rules, but I have no doubt that anywhere in the world scenes may be found that satisfy the requirements. Bonkei, quite obviously, need not be confined to Japan.

I should like to close this introductory chapter by listing, very briefly, the types of bonkei that are available to the creator, based largely on the kind of container that is used and the use to which it is put.

The most orthodox of all the styles is called *suiban* bonkei; the prefix *sui* refers to water, and here water is used to keep the material fresh as well as to give it a sheen. The trays may

Standing Bonkei   Framed Bonkei

be of any size, shape, or material—with the sole proviso, obviously, that they must be waterproof. Most commonly used, therefore, are trays of ceramic, wood, stainless steel, or plastics of various kinds.

In standing bonkei, the tray is customarily leaned against a wall or a rack. It is a style that lends itself particularly well to the depiction of scenes of distant mountains, waterfalls, or deep gorges with the moon floating in the sky. In this bonkei, the sky is often composed of colored sand fixed with paste; then, once the paste is dry, the mountains and rocks can be molded out of *keto* or some other material. The appeal of standing bonkei is remarkably different from that of other styles; the Japanese are fortunate in that they have frequent opportunities to compare the various styles at large bonkei exhibitions, which are held regularly throughout the year.

Hanging bonkei uses *ikebana* vases such as boat-shaped bamboo vessels or half-moon bronzes. These bonkei, like the *ikebana* for which the vases were made, are hung up for viewing either inside the house or out. In summer particularly, when this type of bonkei is hung in the veranda of the house, it seems to freshen the atmosphere and is most attractive.

Framed bonkei is a kind of standing bonkei, with the obvious difference that the bonkei is set into a frame and so may be hung on a wall like a painting. If, as is usually the

27

Table Bonkei   Dry Bonkei

case, dry materials are used (see *kansō* bonkei, p. 118), such as plaster of paris, papier-mâché, and paste, then a framed bonkei will last almost indefinitely, and may be moved, like a painting, from place to place at the whim of the creator.

Another variety is table bonkei and is used, as its name indicates, as a centerpiece. Customarily it is placed so that it may be viewed from all sides, with a waterproof sheet beneath it to protect the surface of the table. This particular type of bonkei is extremely popular with Westerners for whom it is a useful and pleasing expression of Japanese taste.

The standard bonkei, made with *keto* as a base, seldom lasts more than a month. To offset this brief life-span, various substitutes for *keto* have been evolved, as well as special ways of using it. For example, it may be mixed with seaweed, paper, or both, and covered with plaster of paris. In my school, the basic material is usually not *keto* at all, but a mixture of boiled newspaper and clay (called *kansō* bonkei). The result is that the completed work has an enormously prolonged life-span, and so is often used in the creation of framed bonkei.

The reader should take note that I have listed here only the commonest forms of bonkei. In other cases, a wide variety of containers, such as seashells or glass bells may be used. I shall have more to say about this later on.

Chapter 2 TOOLS AND MATERIALS

Some of the tools and much of the material used in Japan have been designed and manufactured expressly for the bonkei artist; the Westerner may, therefore, have difficulty in finding them readily available. After a few experiments, however, he will find suitable substitutes. Thus, he is advised not to take the information given in this chapter too literally but to accept it, rather, as some indication of what is required and to make such substitutions as seem most appropriate. Nor is there any necessity for him to make a formidable investment in tools and materials right at the start: they may be acquired as they are needed.

TOOLS

Trays or other containers
The tray is, of course, indispensable in bonkei. The size most commonly used, as I noted earlier, is about eighteen by six inches and no deeper than an inch; generally the shape is either oval or oblong, and the material is white ceramic. However, for the beginner I would recommend a less ambitious size—something about fourteen inches long by ten

inches wide and about three-quarters of an inch deep. Ikebana trays are not advisable because they are too deep, unless first lined with a false bottom to ensure that the finished bonkei does not seem submerged in its tray. Although a white oblong tray is considered most suitable, this is by no

Multipurpose tray (14½″ long by 9″ wide by ¾″ high)

29

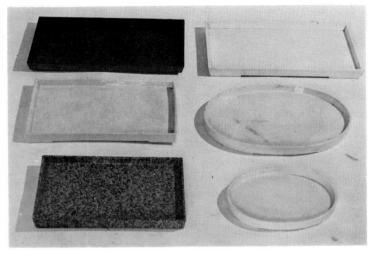
Various types of bonkei trays.

means a fixed rule: a celadon tray or a reddish brown one of some other shape may be preferred. The only essential is that the tray should harmonize with the composition. Trays may be made of artificial stone, for example, or copper, brass, steel, or some other metal, as well as of wood and plastic. For that matter, the bonkei one intends to make may be best suited to a shallow kitchen dish, a tray-shaped flower vessel, a large seashell, or a hanging ikebana tray. One word of caution: if wood is chosen, then it should be lined with

some waterproof material (such as a thin sheet of copper) to prevent leakage. And one word of advice: since a wooden tray can be made in any size, it is eminently suitable for large bonkei creations, but the sides of the tray should be painted white or some very pale color to ensure harmony.

Spatulas
What the brush is to the painter the spatula is to the bonkei expert, who usually has available three different sizes of spatulas made of nickel-coated brass to ensure smoothness. Some artists choose silver spatulas, but these have no particular advantage. For the beginner, one medium-sized spatula (about eight inches long) is sufficient; both faces should be flat and wide, and the handle narrow. The spatula is used to build up mountainous and rocky scenes out of *keto* or a substitute, and to give them their finishing touches. As one's skill increases, the small-sized spatula will probably be found better suited to more detailed work. The biggest of the three is used for large-scale work as well as to separate the *keto* on the tray. I shall have more to say about the use of the spatula in a later chapter.

Ate-ita
Once the final plan for the bonkei has been thought of, the problem arises of how to mold the *keto* or papier-mâché with the spatulas into its ultimate form. The easiest way is to support the material from behind by means of a short

30

wedge (some $3\frac{1}{2}$ inches square) held in one hand, and to shape the material with the other hand, using the spatula you have chosen. This wedge the Japanese call an *ate-ita*. Although it may be made of almost any kind of material, ranging from various kinds of metals (such as aluminum and brass) to plywood and plastics, one made of plastic (celluloid, perhaps) or metal is most suitable, for it is easier to handle.

Sieves

A set of three is necessary, one fine, one coarse, and one with a handle. They have many uses. The sieve with the coarse mesh, for example, is used to sprinkle rough soil, while the fine sieve is for the powder by means of which a snow effect is produced in bonkei. The sieve with a handle is useful for moss (of which more later).

Spoons

Two sizes are desirable, and since their main purpose is to pour sand, ordinary kitchen spoons are sufficient. The beginner will certainly find it unnecessary to buy specially-made bonkei spoons.

Tweezers

These are used for planting moss and small trees and for arranging figures in the finished work, as well as for removing unnecessary bits of *keto*. A pair of tweezers about seven inches long would certainly be adequate.

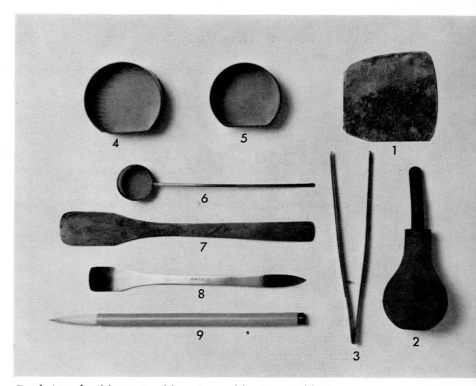

Bonkei tools: (1) *ate-ita*; (2) syringe; (3) pincers; (4) sieve (large); (5) sieve (small); (6) sieve with handle; (7) spatula (large); (8) spatula (small); (9) brush.

Brushes

Three sizes are recommended. (In Japan, we use writing brushes, but I do not consider these a necessity.) The widest brush is used to sweep away small unwanted particles of *keto* and also to level the surface of the sand used to suggest rivers and seas; the bristles of this brush must obviously be kept very dry. The other large brush is used to paint colors on hills and rocks. In Japan it is customary to immerse blocks of color (such as red ochre or rouge) in water, and then to dip the brush into the colored solution—but obviously ingenuity will find an alternative to this process should similar blocks of color be unobtainable. The thin brush is used almost exclusively to paint distant waterfalls white.

Syringes

After the sand used to suggest a river or a sea has been smoothed, water is squirted over it. If the artist feels that there is too much water, he should remove part of it with the syringe or even with an ordinary kitchen spoon. The syringe, incidentally, need not be of the type illustrated in the photograph; an ordinary fountain pen will do.

Mouth-sprayer

This is an implement that may not be familiar to the average Westerner: it is used in Japan to keep ikebana fresh. Equally efficient is the kind of spray or atomiser women use when ironing. Although the usual bonkei made with *keto*

stays fresh for anything between a week and a month, if it is sprayed regularly with water the drying and cracking of the *keto* is retarded and the life of the whole bonkei is prolonged.

Revolving workboard

Although by no means essential, the type of revolving board shown in the photograph is very useful, for it permits the tray to be turned without the artist having to move. The height of the board can be made to suit the convenience of the artist. There is a hole in the middle of the table on which the board is placed, thus allowing it to revolve.

Miscellaneous

Other objects that will be found useful, if not indispensable, are a water container, boxes for powdered pigment, and cleaning rags. Certain schools also use a pointed implement and a special spatula for making forests out of *keto*, while others prefer rubber gloves for landscapes instead of the more conventional *ate-ita* described above.

MATERIALS

The following information refers mainly to schools of bonkei that use *keto* as a primary material, and is not intended to describe other schools that rely chiefly on different materials.

Keto

As I noted earlier, it was not until the mid-Meiji era that the bonkei master, Chisen Izumi, first made use of the ordinary kind of peat called *keto* or *keto-tsuchi*. (It is also known in Japan as *deitan* and *sōtan*.) It is most important that this peat should be composed of the humus of the marsh reed; this has no odor and is generally found at a depth of about six feet below ground. Formerly marshland, the ground has gradually dried, while the *keto* it contains has turned dark brown in color and very light in weight. It has the peculiar property of becoming as malleable as clay when hot water is poured over it. Once it has been molded by the spatula, it retains its shape indefinitely. However, the addition of a little more hot water will render it malleable again and increase both its sheen and its elasticity. It may thus be used over and over again. Furthermore, the dampened *keto* may be preserved in a jar where it is protected from both air and insects. It is thus one of the most economical and useful materials available to the bonkei artist. Peat is found all over the world, but its quality varies depending on the nature of the humus of which it is composed, the climatic conditions of the region, the soil in which it is found, and so on. Not all peat is adaptable for use in bonkei. However, if the reader experiments a bit with the peat that is available at nearby florists and nurseries, he will probably discover one or more varieties with the particular qualities that bonkei demands. If he does not, there are various substitutes available to him. In fact, the Japanese bonkei artist often prefers one or other of the substitutes to dry *keto* itself.

The making of keto:
1) Type of reeds from which it is ultimately obtained.

2) After rotting and lying in the soil for a long time, *keto* turns into a dark brown mass of humus mixed with rough fibers. Once dried, it is very light in weight. Shown here is *keto* as it is sold in bonkei supply shops. 3) First stage in its preparation, when either hot or cold water is poured over it. 4) It is then thoroughly mixed until it takes on a clay-like quality. 5) The mixing is best done in a large container or on a stone floor, and results in a lump of *keto* of great elasticity. 6) It should eventually be made into five or six lumps about the size of a tennis ball. These are placed in the appropriate position on the tray. 7) Out of them may be formed mountains, rocks, islands, hills, and plains.

MATERIALS

(Right top to bottom)
Artificial moss: yellowish green, green, dark green, yellow, orange, red. Wave sand; snow powder; sea sand (*mazuna* dyed blue); wave sand dyed light blue; wave sand dyed dark blue; sand for road; *oiso* (the largest-grained sand); *chuiso* (medium-sized grains); *koiso* (fine-grained sand).

(Top left to right)
hakudo (white clay); *benigara* (colcothar—a red dye); *tonoko* (light brown powdered pigment); bluish-green dye; chrome yellow and dark green dye (when mixed giving dark green).

Below each saucer is shown the color of the final solution when mixed with water.

keto (peat)

35

LIVING TREES (*left to right*)
box trees (left two); eleocharis; five-needled pine tree; Japanese andromeda; cryptomeria; juniper; *himuro sugi* (chamaecyparis pisifera); fire thorn; azalea; cedar.

TYPES OF LIVING GRASS, MOSS, AND ROCK PLANTS USED IN BONKEI

EXAMPLES OF ARTIFICIAL TREES AND FLOWERS

Papier-mâché is frequently used as a base for bonkei and in a finished work is often indistinguishable from *keto*. Newspaper is crumpled up and put in a basin, where boiling water is poured over it; after it has cooled, it is kneaded until it forms a solid mass. Then excess water is removed, and sifted clay is added. Proportions vary, naturally, depending on the effect desired; so here again the novice is advised to experiment until he is at home with the material and can alter the proportions to suit his needs. Two other useful substitutes for *keto* have been developed recently: *keito* and *keiso*. These are made of either white clay (*hakudo*) or a clay-like soil, to which rough fibers and water have been added. The resulting mixture may be used in the same way as *keto*.

Hakudo

A grayish white powder, this can also be dissolved in water until it has the texture of thick soup and then applied with a spatula to suggest the wrinkles that are found in mountains, hills, and rocks. In the same way, dark rocky areas and sharp summits can be made to stand out in bold relief.

Benigara

This reddish brown pigment in powder form, called colcothar, is dissolved in seven to ten parts of water to make a usable solution. For example, after a mountain has been built out of *keto* and finishing touches have been applied with *hakudo*, then the surface may be accented by painting sections of it with *benigara*. The contrast between the green of trees on mountains in the middle or far distance and the red of rocks jutting out from amongst them is well emphasized by this treatment. (*See color plate on page 35.*)

Tonoko

A solution of this powder (which is a yellowish brown dye mixed with a little clay) is made up to about the same density as *benigara* and has various uses in bonkei such as painting brightly polished swords, wooden fittings in buildings, and the rocky surfaces of mountains in the relative foreground. (*See plate on page 35.*)

Hakudo (an ash-white powdered clay dissolved in water) is applied to *keto*-formed mountains and rocks with a spatula to simulate creases in the rocks.

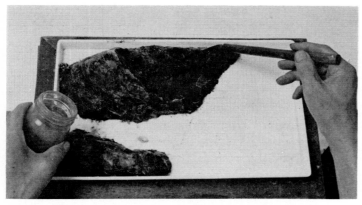

Solutions of *benigara* (red), *tonoko* (brown), and verdigris (green or blue green) are then added to simulate the folds in mountains. The technique is to touch the mountain lightly with a brush dipped in the solution, allowing it to drip down the slopes.

Verdigris

There are two types of this green solution: one in which a blue powder has been dissolved; the other in which yellow lead (*ōen*) is mixed with purple (*kinpero*). The latter is always to be preferred when available. The solution has the density of *benigara* and *tonoko*, and after these have been applied to the bonkei, it is used primarily to give intensity to the green of trees on distant mountains and to the grass and moss on mountains in the foreground. (*See color plate on page 35.*)

White poster paint

This is used to give the illusion of a waterfall on a distant mountain. (One general remark, already noted, is that the colors in bonkei must always be muted.)

Artificial moss (*maki-goke*)

This extremely useful material comes in many shades of green (and other colors), although only three greens are in general use: medium green, dark green, and yellow green. (*See color plate on page 35.*) In powder form, it may be sprinkled on distant mountains and hills to give the illusion of forests, or on landscapes in the foreground to suggest moss and grass as well as low bushes. It can also be used in combination with natural moss; after the latter is placed in the landscape, the artificial moss is sprinkled nearby to simulate trees and bushes. The medium green moss, called *hongoke*, is used to represent the average landscape (*color plate on page 35*). The yellow green variety, on the other hand, is intended to suggest a sunny landscape or one facing in a southerly direction (*color plate on page 35*); yellow green moss may also serve to represent young leaves and new grass. Dark green moss would be used for a landscape facing north or to suggest a swampy region. Correct use of this artificial moss gives a particularly soft quality to a bonkei. Usually, it is sprinkled through a sieve, but where only a touch of it is desired, it should be placed by hand.

Other powders are also called *maki-goke*; these, although not moss-colored, are used in a similar way. The three most commonly used to accompany the green mosses mentioned above are yellow, vermilion, and scarlet (*see color plate on page 35*); their purpose is to suggest such familiar flora as rape, azalea, cherry blossom, maple, and the like. Note that these powders are not sprinkled directly onto the landscape, but rather onto other materials (such as moss, grass, and twigs) that have been arranged to simulate fields of cherry trees, maples, or azaleas.

Powdered gypsum
This is sprinkled through a sieve to represent snow on distant mountains, and, though not indispensable, is better than any substitutes (like lime). (*See color plate on page 35.*)

Sand
A number of different kinds of sand, as well as imitation sand, are widely used in bonkei and bonseki. One, called *nami-suna*, is made of powdered calcite or marble and is used to represent high waves breaking on the shore, for example, or rushing streams. Since bonkei usually depicts turbulent rather than still water in its seascapes, *nami-suna* is essential. It gives life to the water. However, it is not easy to use and the beginner will find that it will take him a certain time to learn how to create lifelike waves out of sand. (*See color plate on page 35.*)

Powdered artificial moss is scattered by hand or through a sieve. Three shades of green are in general use.

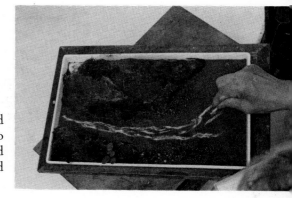

Very fine white sand is added to the coarser blue sand to suggest waves on the sea and on rivers. It is usually applied with the fingertips.

Another type of sand in frequent use is found both on the seashore and in river beds. In Japan it is dyed blue and is used to represent expanses of water—seas, rivers, and swamps. The technique is to transfer it to the tray by means of a spoon, then pour water over it and shake the tray slightly so as to make the surface level and smooth. (*See color plate on page 35.*)

Mazuna is also found both on seashores and in river beds but is an extremely fine sand. It is, therefore, commonly used only for rivers and lakes, never for seas or oceans. For this reason, *mazuna* is often called "river sand." The technique for using it is exactly the same as that given in the preceding paragraph.

This sand is also tinted various shades of blue in order to suggest the state of the weather, the distance of the water from the viewer, and its depth. Light blue, for example, is appropriate for a distant body of water or for one that is nearby but shallow (*see plate on page 35*), while a darker blue is used for deep water (*plate on page 35*).

Another type of sand altogether is *michisuna* (which is also called *negishi*), a brown sand used for roads and mountain paths. It is customary to sprinkle the large, rough grains by hand and to use a sieve for the smaller grains. (*See color plate on page 35.*)

Isosuna is also used for seascapes and riverbanks as well as for any sort of shallow water. Its grains tend to be large, rough and mixed in color, depending on the place of origin:

Sand dyed blue serves to represent various bodies of water—seas, rivers, and lakes—depending on the size of the grain. It is usually spooned into the tray, and water is poured over it to make the surface level.

Brown sand is used to suggest roads as well as the ground in and around villages. The sieve is used for small grains, while larger grains are scattered by hand.

This sand has a larger grain than that shown on the preceding page and is used for riverbeds and seashores. Progressively smaller grains should be used nearer the water.

Innumerable varieties of living moss are used in bonkei, the larger plants generally being placed in the foreground, the smaller ones in the distance to suggest forests.

some, for instance, are blue-black and white, others brown and white. Ōiso beach (in Kanagawa Prefecture) is generally considered to supply the best *isosuna*, and for that reason this particular sand is often referred to as *ōisosuna*. In Japan, according to the size of the grain, it is divided into three types, called *ōiso (color plate on page 35)*, *chūiso (color plate on page 35)*, and *koiso (color plate on page 35)*. *Chūiso* is commonly used for the shore itself, while *koiso* is considered more suitable for any sort of shallow water, and *ōiso* for more distant water. Here again, experimentation and ingenuity will supply substitutes.

Soil
Widely used in bonkei (for gardens, fields, mounds and suchlike), is a rich brown soil that may be bought already prepared (at least in Japan), but which the artist can easily prepare for himself. All one need do is dry the soil well, then grind it into a powder, passing it through a fine sieve.

Natural flora
The skilled bonkei artist makes use of a wide variety of small plants and miniature trees (bonsai) as well as grass and moss. Since a landscape consisting solely of seedlings would not be very interesting, the bonkei artist, when he finds an attractive seedling in the country or the mountains, after uprooting it and carrying it home, may keep it for some time before making use of it. Small, well-shaped trees best suited

to bonkei are cedar, boxwood, pine, plum, abelia, larix, bamboo, and spirea. Certain grasses, like zoysia, and small wild flowers, like St.-John's-wort, are also favored. Numerous varieties of bamboo are also extremely useful, while natural moss is as indispensable as the artificial moss mentioned earlier. A little natural moss, for instance, placed on a distant mountain, will make the mountain appear to be bursting with life. The bonkei artist must be aware of the tremendous possibilities inherent in the many varieties of moss available to him. (*See color plate on page 36.*)

Artificial flora
Our school prefers to make use of living bonsai with roots, since they impart a vitality to the bonkei that no artificial substitute could provide. At the same time, we recognize that artificial trees and flowers can be not only useful but on occasion indispensable, particularly for dry bonkei, since they may be preserved for a long period of time and used over and over again. It is for these reasons that some bonkei schools use artificial flora almost exclusively. One method that combines the natural and the artificial might be mentioned here. It consists of using the thin roots of a tree as its trunk and branches, to which artificial leaves are attached with some adhesive. The roots themselves are bound together by means of wire to form the tree. Once again, Japanese shops have these objects for sale, but they are fun to make for oneself, and not very difficult. Tree trunks may also be

formed of *keto* (or papier-mâché), after which they are "planted" in the landscape by boring a hole in it with a gimlet. (*See color plate on page 36.*)

Ornaments
The variety of miniature objects that may be incorporated into a bonkei is endless—as is the source of supply. A skilled potter will probably make and paint his own figures—farmers, fishermen, domestic animals, and the like. Otherwise, a toy shop will prove an inexhaustible supply; and it is likely that the figures will need repainting to ensure harmony with the rest of the composition. If a farmhouse or a bridge is part of your landscape, then you will almost certainly want to make your own merely by glueing small strips of wood together. Or you may want to build a lighthouse and place it high on a rugged cliff or make a fleet of fishing boats and decide whether they are to sail a calm sea or not. As long as the rule of harmony is adhered to, multicolored objects will give added life and excitement to your composition.

There is no end to the kinds of ornaments that ▷ may be used in bonkei—from human figures and animals to boats, bridges, towers, and houses. They may be made of almost any material, and their size generally determines their location.

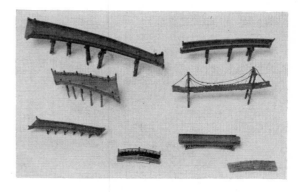

Chapter 3 SOME BASIC CONSIDERATIONS

No one who has ever looked at a painting is unaware of the fundamental fact that its artist usually begins with an idea. It may be nebulous at first and sharpen only after a period of time, minutes or years, or it may burst upon him with total clarity at the initial moment of impact. In either case, it is usually only after the idea is clear in his mind that he undertakes to develop it into a composition. Obviously, both the original conception as well as the way in which it is carried out must lie well within the artist's range if the completed work is to be of any merit. All these self-evident observations apply to bonkei as truly as they do to painting.

SELECTING THEMES

Themes, however, are more limited, for most bonkei masters have chosen to depict natural landscapes or seascapes, employing for the most part mountains and valleys, fields, seas, and rivers. (There would seem to be no law against an abstract, surrealist, or expressionist bonkei, but the fact remains that—at least in Japan—bonkei artists have confined themselves to a faithful, albeit personal, representation of

nature; and the novice in any country would be well advised to follow their example.) What the Japanese masters have lacked in latitude they have attempted to compensate for by a sense of drama: that is why they have so often chosen to depict nature in one of its more violent or spectacular moments.

First, of course, the artist must "see" the scene that he intends to reproduce. Then, to a certain extent, he must rearrange it in his own mind, so that the finished product is not merely a sterile reproduction of some natural scene. This process obviously involves determining the position of the elements of the composition: where the mountains and rivers are to lie, where the sea is to meet the shore, where the trees are to be planted.

The beginner is therefore advised to try his hand at scenes that he may well consider hackneyed. In Japan, he would be set to doing views of Fuji or the famous pine groves at Miho. Western equivalents might be the Alps, or Stonehenge, or the Hudson River above New York, or—if the artist is extremely ambitious—the Grand Canyon. Having chosen such a familiar scene, the trick is to personalize it to ensure that one expresses one's own personality as well as the scene before one's eyes. With the master, this ability to mingle self and nature in order to produce an original creation is almost automatic. One word of caution is that, because a dramatic landscape expressing the grandeur of nature is preferred in bonkei, the beginner may be led into making a complicated and intricate landscape. It is clear, though, that to compress into a small tray all the elements of nature at its most sublime is an impossible task. Therefore, the landscape should be as simple as possible and yet retain the impression of grandeur. No easy task, but a necessary one if the completed work is to express the artist's own reaction to the beauty of a scene without departing from that sense of harmony which is the essence of bonkei.

Once the artist has mastered the use of the tools, familiarized himself with the nature of the materials, and acquired the ability to express his own personality however familiar the scene, he is free to make any sort of bonkei. He may follow the example of the masters or make his own rules: in any case, the final work will exhibit some elements of ancient Japanese art, however infused they may be with contemporary ideas.

The beginner as well as the master will find it helpful when travelling through the country to carry either a sketch-pad or a camera (or both). To make a sketch of a scene that may eventually be transformed into a bonkei does not re-quire the talent of an accomplished artist; a rough draft of the scene will serve as some reminder when the time comes to make the bonkei. A sketch gives form to one's visual impression—an invaluable aid in the planning of the final composition.

A photograph may also be extremely useful, though in a different way. Since the camera merely records, it does not look instinctively, as the human eye does, for harmony and relationship, nor does it register the strength of the impression that various aspects of a scene may make on the human brain. Nevertheless, it is an extremely valuable aid, and in a later chapter I shall go into the subject of how best to use a photograph as the basis for a bonkei.

COMPOSITION

The chief point about the art of bonkei is the fact that it aspires to recreate the grandeur of nature within the confines of a small tray, in order to do which it must impart a sense of distance. This it accomplishes through the use of a three-dimensional structure, usually making clear distinctions between near, middle, and far distant areas. In the accompanying sketch (*page 45*), for example, the summit of Mount Fuji rises high in the distance, the mountains of Hakone lie in the middle, and the foreground is occupied by trees.

Not all bonkei have three such sharply delineated areas. Some, in fact, have only one; others have two; and it is customary to categorize a bonkei according to the number of areas it contains. Whatever the number, however, the harmony that is the essence of bonkei will not be easily achieved. Simple though his composition may be, the artist will find it a challenging task to carry out.

His first step, whether he is working from memory, from a photograph, or from nature itself, is to make a sketch of the landscape or seascape he hopes to recreate in his own idiom. This preliminary sketch, however rough, is essential

Example of a one-scene bonkei.

Example of a two-scene bonkei.

46

—especially in making clear to the artist himself the distinctions between distant, middle, and foreground areas, so that the final result will give the effect of an effortless and natural three-dimensionality.

The fundamental rule in composing a Japanese bonkei is to divide the surface of the tray into ten equal parts, as shown in Diagram A on page 47; the way in which these parts are divided will make it easier to determine whether the main emphasis is on the foreground, the middle scene, or the far distance.

The basic composition for a three-scene bonkei is shown in Diagram B on page 48, but there are obviously other possibilities, since the artist must be free to find the most suitable, harmonious, and perhaps dramatic composition for the landscape that he is attempting to depict. Diagrams C, D, and E (*pages 48–49*) show how best to arrange the composition in order to emphasize (1) the near scene, (2) the middle scene, and (3) the distant scene.

In Diagram C, for example, the ratio of the three scenes, from distant to near, is two, three, and five; in Diagram D, it is two, five, and three; while in Diagram E, it is four, three, and three. Obviously, these ratios can be changed

Example of a three-scene bonkei.

Diagram A: Dividing the tray into ten equal parts.

when the composition requires it, but the beginner is urged to follow them until he is sufficiently adept to make changes without spoiling his bonkei.

Three examples are also given in which the area of the tray is divided into only two parts (*diagrams F, G, and H, pages 50–51*). F shows a bonkei with a distant and mid-distant scene; G, a mid-distant and foreground scene; and H, a foreground and far distant scene. The intention behind all the varying ratios is to impart that sense of distance which is essential to three-dimensionality.

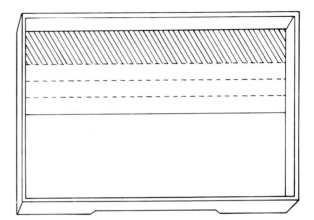

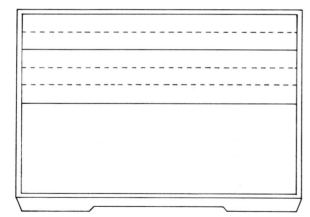

Diagram B: Basic composition for a three-scene bonkei.

Diagram C: Basic composition emphasizing the foreground, with example of finished bonkei.

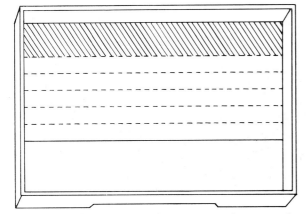

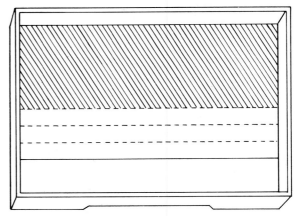

Diagram D: Basic composition emphasizing the middle scene, with example of finished bonkei.

Diagram E: Basic composition emphasizing the distant scene, with example of finished bonkei.

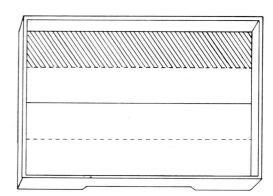

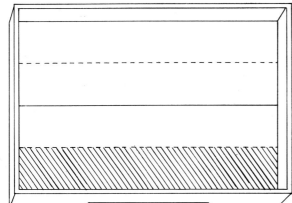

Diagram F: Basic composition for distant and mid-distant scene, with example of completed bonkei.

Diagram G: Basic composition for mid-distant and foreground scene, with example of completed bonkei.

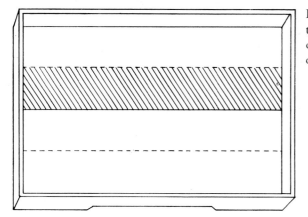

Diagram H: Basic composition for foreground and distant scene, with example of completed bonkei.

To that end the artist must attempt to arrange his various components with the utmost skill. Distant forests are suggested by means of moss, near ones by small *bonsai* trees. The same is true, of course, of such ornamental additions as houses and boats: large ones in the foreground, small ones in the distance. In the case of mountains, there are no fixed rules when they occur in mid-distant and foreground areas; but when they appear in the far distance, the Japanese bonkei artist distinguishes between three different types of mountains:

1. Those that rise high in the sky.
2. Those that tower over a plain.
3. Those with deep valleys.

There are various ways of deciding upon your final composition. One particularly recommended to the beginner is to cut out pictures of mountains, rocks, fields, and seacoasts, for example, and move them about on the tray until a satisfactory composition is reached. Another method is to make a paper cutout like that shown on page 51, which may be used to determine how much of a photograph you want to use for the final composition, or, in the case of a natural landscape, by holding the cutout up in front of you, to eliminate the extraneous parts of the scene.

Here are a few more words of practical advice that should prove useful to the beginner. If, as is customary, there are three areas in your bonkei, then one of them must unmistakably predominate. It serves, so to speak, as the focal point, the chief point of interest on which the viewer's eye first falls.

I think of this chief scene as the title role of the bonkei drama; the secondary scene then becomes a supporting role; and the third scene provides the harmony and the essential balance between the two. Take the "View of Tsukuba," for example, (*diagram lower left*). Here the title role is Mount Tsukuba itself, in the distance; the supporting role is the mountain range in the middle area; while the trees, grass, and ornaments in the foreground link the two together. It is important to determine which area is to play the leading part: if there is any uncertainty on that point, then the whole bonkei will suffer. There must be no question, in the immediate reaction of the viewer, as to which area is the chief point of interest in any particular bonkei.

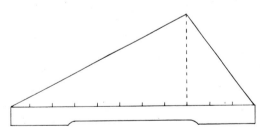

The chief point of interest is never central; it always lies either to right or left of center.

If the beginner decides on a high, distant mountain as his chief point of interest, then his immediate reaction will be to place it centrally. This would be a mistake, for he would succeed only in dividing his bonkei sharply in two, losing all hope of achieving total harmony. Only after he has divided his tray into tenths and thus determined upon the area of primary interest will he be able to decide how far to right or left of center that high, distant mountain should lie. The advice I give the pupils in my school is to use the scalene rather than the equilateral triangle, for it is only with the former that the harmony we are seeking can be achieved. My advice is also to make sure that the height of the mountain is in proportion to the other elements of the bonkei: the tendency of the beginner when taking a tall, distant mountain as his focal point is to make it too tall, thus destroying the symmetry of his work.

Very often the artist will find that there is one particular place in his bonkei, and no other, where, by placing a stone, a tree, or some similar object, he not only emphasizes the chief point of interest but also helps to make the whole bonkei come alive. The Japanese term for these stones and trees might be best rendered in English as "strategic," because of their tremendous importance in bonkei. Placing such objects "strategically" is one of the knacks that the skilled bonkei artist must acquire. Examples might be a large stone placed with a sufficient sense of distance in front of a fisherman's cottage to protect it from the waves; or a tree beside a mountain chalet; or either a rock or a tree at both ends of a bridge to prevent it looking unpleasantly bare and alien in the landscape.

In Japan, a large tree is customarily placed beside a house to protect it from the wind.

Mountains

In the case of mountains (examples of which may be seen throughout the book), the artist should constantly beware of making them lean forward—a position that the viewer would find oppressive and disagreeable (the same is true of large trees). Furthermore, if your mountain rises high into the sky above a flat plain, try to avoid (at least at first) forms like some of the needlelike peaks of the Alps and other mountains that rise almost perpendicularly, and make your mountain look as natural as possible by having it slope gradually downward.

Valleys and rocks

Deep valleys between cliffs can be bare, snow-covered, or forested—probably the last is easiest for the beginner to handle. In the case of huge rocks, one side should always form a steep cliff.

As far as possible, it is wise to avoid duplicating the shapes of any of the elements in a particular bonkei, whether they are mountains, valleys, rivers, roads, or islands. Duplication of this sort impairs the composition of a bonkei, and although nature itself may duplicate, the artist must not allow himself a similar freedom. For the same reason, rocks jutting out from the surface of the sea, or rocks at the sea's edge, should be of many different sizes; furthermore, the artist will find that odd rather than even numbers of rocks make a better composition. (The same is true, incidentally,

of trees.) Even in the case of distant mountains, where duplication of shapes would seem to be of little importance, it should be avoided as much as possible.

Rivers

There are a few general rules about rivers that will seem obvious, but which are, nevertheless, important enough. The first, and most obvious, is that an utterly straight river is not of great interest, while an S-shaped river (like the Seine in Paris) is pleasing to the eye. Of little interest also are rivers that run parallel to each other; the artist should limit himself strictly to a maximum of two. To help create the illusion

Try to avoid duplication of form and make rivers, as well as roads, winding rather than straight.

54

of distance, the upper reaches of a river should be narrow, and it should widen as it approaches the foreground. (These rules are illustrated on page 111.) The same considerations apply to roads—with one further condition: it is wise to avoid roads that cross one another as this generally confuses the perspective. In the case of rivers, the source ought to be indicated, if possible, by means of trees or rocks.

Ornaments

Ornaments, such as houses and boats, should naturally be of different sizes, so that the largest occupy the foreground while the smallest are tucked skillfully away in the farthest distance, with the others in between. The same is true of grass, with the tallest blades being placed in the foreground. Broad-leaved trees, as I mentioned earlier, also go in the foreground, while those with smaller leaves are kept for distant scenes.

Waves

Using sand to depict water, it should be kept in mind that even on the calmest days a slight breeze will cause ripples farther out and waves where the sea strikes the shore. The illusion of water would be hard to create if the water were motionless. In any case the more you experiment with the technique of making sand look like moving water, the more fascinated you will be by the problems involved.

SEASONS

Another intriguing problem is how to suggest the time of year, for not only are there four seasons but there are variations within them. If you want to depict a landscape in late summer, for example, then you will not want to suggest early autumn to the viewer. The distinctions are subtle but important, for bonkei, as we have noted, is essentially a landscape art, and except in a few seasonless places like the tropics, a landscape that does not suggest the time of year is indeed an unnatural sight. The signs used—snow patches on a distant mountain, a swollen river, yellowing grass, bare trees—must depend, obviously, on the place where you are working. But the signs must be there if the bonkei is to have a life of its own. And, of course, seasonal flowers can always be used (such as the chrysanthemum or the rose, for example), or seasonal holidays (Halloween, Christmas, Midsummer Day), or seasonal activities (skiing as opposed to swimming) to further indicate the time of year. Masters of the art can even, with only a few strokes of the spatula, make a distant mountain further the illusion, but the beginner is advised to use more obvious signs. Look, for example, at the photograph on page 17 entitled "Mount Fuji by the Lake-Side." Since the time of year is spring, the predominant color is light green, with a liberal use of artificial moss and seasonal flowers. The same bonkei, however, can be turned into a winter landscape by tilting the front of the tray a little upwards and spraying the scene with snow powder—thickly on the mountain, thinly on the trees and lake. Ceremonial bonkei, such as those made for funerals, weddings, or birthdays, ought also, obviously, to suggest the time of year of the event being celebrated.

TITLES

As far as the title for a bonkei is concerned, there is little to be said. A title might come to mind before work is started or during the process of creation; it might also be the result of long study after the bonkei has been completed. I myself believe that the bonkei-maker is well-advised not to be too literal in his titles, lest the viewer make immediate comparisons with the original and find disturbing differences. A less precise, more imaginative title will, on the other hand, give further scope for imagination—and that, after all, is one of the prime reasons for making a bonkei: to let the viewer enter through a real landscape into an imaginary world where imperfections in the original scene have been eliminated.

KEEPING BONKEI FRESH

As I noted earlier, the length of time a bonkei will last depends largely on the materials used. A completely dry bonkei, made of papier-mâché and using artificial flora, will last almost indefinitely, while the average life-span of a bonkei made of *keto* is about one month.

But since one of the chief attractions of a bonkei is its freshness, *keto*, despite its short life, must be considered su-

perior to lifeless yet more durable materials. Even to keep a *keto* bonkei looking fresh for a month is no easy task. Unless it is sprayed with water about twice a day, the mountains and rocks will shrink and crack, while the living elements in the bonkei will die. The sand representing bodies of water must also be regularly resupplied with water to preserve the freshness of its appearance.

There are a few rules that will help prolong the life of a living bonkei, perhaps even up to six months if the bonkei-maker is extremely clever and patient:

1. If the bonkei is kept outdoors, the water in the tray should be changed once every five days.

2. Preferable to ordinary tap water is the special kind of water that pet fish like.

3. Since the color of the paint used on mountains and rocks changes in about ten days, it is wise to repaint them weekly with similar pigments and then resprinkle them with artificial moss.

4. If the sand denoting expanses of water seems to be changing in color, sprinkle fresh sand over it through a sieve.

Does this seem like a lot of work just to keep a bonkei looking fresh? You will find that it is not, once you have created a bonkei that pleases you. You will want to keep it looking as fresh as the day you finished it for as long as possible. In any case, it does not require daily rearrangement as does *ikebana*.

Once its life has come to a natural end, dismantle the bonkei carefully. First take off the ornaments and put them away. Then cautiously remove the trees (whose roots have been wrapped in newspaper) and replant them in the original *bonsai* tray. The living moss may also be replanted. The sand should be dried, passed through a sieve and stored. The last to come out is the *keto*. First, using a dry brush, remove the moss and colored sand that have been sprinkled over it. Then crush it in your hands, or, if it is very hard, wrap it in a cloth and pound it into powder with a wooden mallet. You can then pour hot water over it and remold it. If you want to increase its volume, add bits of paper. Probably the easiest way to store it, if you are not going to use it again immediately, is in a plastic bag.

One practical consideration the beginner must bear in mind is that, if living materials have been used, they should be kept fresh with water—thus necessitating drainage. One method is to leave space at the rear of the tray—behind distant mountains, for example—where excess water can collect. If the tray is then tilted slightly, the water may be removed with a syringe.

In the diagram, another method for dealing with drainage is shown. Before a composition is planned and space allocated, a small board should be placed beneath the tray, and cloth, newspaper, absorbent cotton, or some similar material laid over it. Build your bonkei on top, and after it is complete bore a hole in the board through which water may be drained away.

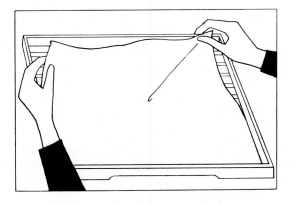

Chapter 4   THE USE OF THE SPATULA

It is difficult to give precise instructions as to how to use the spatula most effectively without an actual demonstration. Nonetheless, it is the chief tool in the repertoire of the bonkei artist; the novice must, therefore, acting on the hints given below, experiment until he is satisfied that he has mastered its techniques. He should not be dismayed at the prospect, for, although these techniques are not easy, they do not compare in complexity with the varied uses of the brush which the painter must learn before he can feel that he truly knows his art—if, indeed, he ever feels that he does. The challenge of painting frequently outlasts a painter's life: Titian, when nearly a hundred, was still developing new techniques. The challenge of bonkei is of a different nature, and does not require the same, single-minded dedication as painting. It is an easier medium to work in, yet it can never be mastered without complete dexterity in the use of the spatula. The spatula is, in that sense, the key to bonkei.

First of all, the artist must ensure that, whether he chooses to sit or stand as he works, the tray on its pedestal is at a suitable and comfortable height and distance, so that unhampered movements with both hands and arms may be made when working directly on the tray. Much preparation, however, as we have noted, is done on the workboard. In view of this, since most people are right-handed, it is customary to hold the spatula in the right hand, just below the middle of the handle, and the wedge (*ate-ita*) in the left. The roles of the hands may, of course, be reversed, depending on the artist, but he must be sure that his posture is neither cramped nor uncomfortable. He must have freedom of movement lest the shapes of his mountains and his rocks reflect his lack of it.

The basic strokes of the spatula used to express variations in mountainous surfaces are customarily divided into four categories (*shown in the diagram on page 59*): cone-shaped strokes, horizontal strokes, vertical strokes, and slanting strokes. My recommendation to the learner is that, using *keto* and a spatula, he should practise these four different types of strokes until he feels he is proficient at all of them.

The photograph below the diagram on the same page shows the four types of mountainous surfaces with the all-important added indication of white lines, using the tip of the spatula dipped in a solution of *hakudo* (white clay). It is important to bear in mind that neither horizontal nor vertical lines can be adequately indicated by merely moving the spatula either straight up or straight down. Nature is not generally so simple, and the lines made by the spatula should reflect its complexities.

In general, the initial technique for the creation of a mountain is to take a lump of *keto*, wrap it in newspaper, and mold it by hand into roughly the desired shape. Then remove the newspaper and with the tip of the spatula add the solution of white clay, which is essential to denote the convolutions of a mountainous surface, thus obtaining, through the unevenness of the surface, the required sense of realism. The precise shade of color of the solution you are using must be taken into account, and unpainted surfaces are just as important as painted ones. The solution ought to be sufficiently thick not to drip down the slopes of the mountain immediately after it is applied with the tip of spatula but rather a few seconds later. On the other hand, it must not be so thick that it sticks to the spatula and soon coagulates. You will find it necessary to stir, check, and probably correct the density of the solution from time to time as you work.

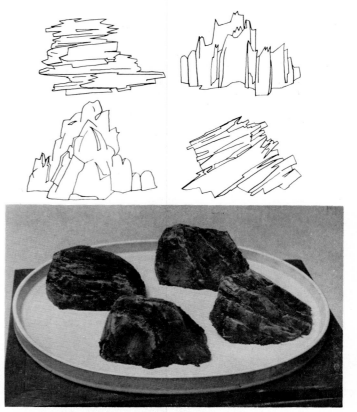

Examples of horizontal strokes (left rear); vertical strokes (right rear); cone-shaped strokes (front left); and slanting strokes (front right).

59

Cone-shaped Strokes

Almost invariably, as I have noted, the bonkei artist initially takes a lump of *keto* of the required size, wraps it in newspaper, and places it on the board, where he does the preliminary modelling by hand. Then, having removed the newspaper, he pushes the whole face of the spatula up and then down until the mountain has taken shape.

It is only then that he adds the white-clay solution with the tip of the spatula to suggest the folds of the mountain's surface. A conical mountain is shown being formed in photographs 1–4 on at right, where white clay is applied using largely the face of the spatula and following the contours of the mountain. In the case of mountains formed with either horizontal or vertical strokes, the same initial process is followed; it is only in the application of the white-clay solution that the technical processes vary.

60

HORIZONTAL STROKES

To make horizontal lines indicating the layers of rock, hold the spatula in a vertical position, apply it to the *keto*, and draw it across, making as many such layers as is proportionate to the height of the mountain. Having done so, apply the spatula horizontally to the layers, moving it up or down or sideways in order to create clear breaks such as are found in nature. Then paint the breaks, using the same white-clay solution on the tip of the spatula. The various layers should now be sharply delineated.

61

VERTICAL STROKES

Vertical strokes are intended to stand out more prominently than horizontal ones. Therefore, having created the lines by applying the spatula, held in a vertical position, against the *keto* and drawing it up, you now paint in the lines with the white-clay solution, achieving contrast by means of dark and light touches. This latter operation is one of the few occasions when the face of the spatula is preferred to the back, although since the thick white-clay solution adheres to both sides of the spatula, you need not confine yourself solely to one side. One further consideration in the making of vertical folds is that the reverse side of the spatula is generally used in a down-up movement on the left face of the mountain, while in the making of the right face the back of the spatula would be fairly difficult to manipulate, so the front side is customarily used instead. (*See photographs 1–5 on pages 62 and 63.*)

4

5

SLANTING STROKES

To create seashores, rocks jutting out into the sea, and the like, the *keto* may be pressed directly to the tray with a spatula. In this case, oblique lines and strokes will be found highly useful. The spatula is held horizontally to form the initial shape, then vertically to incise the oblique lines, while the *hakudo* may be applied with the edge of the spatula, which is very thin. (*See photographs 1–6 on pages 63 and 64.*) There are a few other facts the bonkei artist should bear in mind when approaching the task of creating mountains in a small tray. For one thing, every mountain has an individual form. Its shape is unique, its very personality is unique—and this factor must be communicated by the successful bonkei artist. The mountain should be *seen* as clearly as possible, then sketched, however roughly, in such a way as to enable its recreation in miniature in a tray.

1

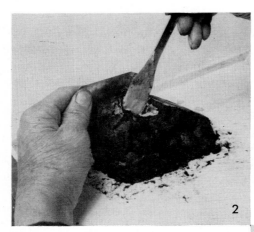

Distant Mountains

Experience has proved that a single, distant mountain in bonkei ought generally to be slender, since only about twenty percent of the space on a tray can be allocated to the distant scene. If the artist hopes to create distant ranges, then he must take great care when painting them with white clay, since it is the shades of color of the clay that will help further not only the illusion of distance but also the all-important one of perspective. The artist would be well-advised to think of distant mountains as though the distant scene itself were divided into distant, middle distant, and foreground scenes: thus he will avoid not only monotony but also the failure to suggest great distances.

Middle Distant Mountains

Mountains in the middle distance ought to be more massive than those of the far distance, and the folds should be made deeper through the simple expedient of putting more clay-powder solution on the spatula, while mountains in the foreground should be most deeply creased of all—if only to suggest the ruggedness that is always associated with high mountains.

Foreground Mountains

In the foreground, it is important to distinguish between rocks and the bare surface of a mountain. Furthermore, depending on the type of landscape you are creating, the foothills of mountains in the foreground may be rocks, cliffs, or even level land. For example, in cases where the mountain towers over the nearby sea, its lower regions may be cliffs; where it adjoins level land, a field of rushes may serve to outline the foothills. As always, ornaments of various kinds can be used to suggest the time of year.

One extremely important factor is that, in the making of mountains, the artist should use a single lump of *keto*. He should begin with a larger amount than he anticipates he will require and scrape it down to the desired size. He should never attempt to increase the size of the mountain by adding more *keto*: the result would inevitably be unattractive.

It is important to remember also that, in bonkei, should the artist place mountains in all the three areas, or in only two, he must in some way create a relationship between them. He ought not to treat them as though they were two or three isolated rows: the space between them should, in one way or another, be filled. The viewer must feel that (*as shown in diagram A, as opposed to diagram B, on page 67*) it would be possible to move from one mountain to another.

Mountains in the far distance, middle distance, and foreground.

1. A far distant mountain. Notice that it is quite narrow in form, and that it decreases in height towards the far side of the tray to further the sense of depth.

2. Mountains in the middle distance should be rounder and somewhat more deeply creased.

3. Distant and mid-distant mountains seen from above.

4. Foreground mountains have the deepest folds and the roughest surface.

5. Mountains in the three areas as seen from above. Valleys between mountains should not be too deep.

66

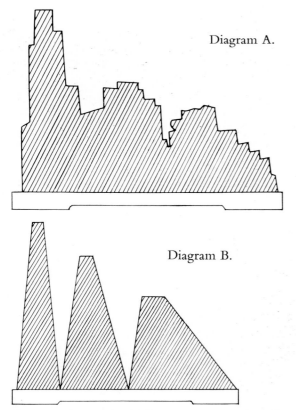

Diagram A.

Diagram B.

The viewer's eye should be able to move effortlessly from one range to another, as shown in Diagram A; Diagram B illustrates valleys that have been made too deep.

ROCKS

In the making of rocks, the process is similar to that used for mountains. The initial shape is molded from a lump of *keto* on the workboard. Then the basic horizontal, vertical, or slanting strokes are employed to express the particular characteristics of the rock. It is only then that the artist has recourse to the white-clay solution to suggest the folds in rocks. (*See photograph 1 on page 68.*) The contrast between the ash-white clay solution and the dark *keto* is particularly effective in the making of sharp-edged, rough-surfaced rocks; depending on the degree of roughness desired, therefore, the quantity of white clay to be used should be very carefully guaged.

When making a rock of relatively smooth surface, the whole face of the spatula should be used. A more weathered and angular surface requires deeper and sharper strokes, so the tip of the spatula is used (*see photograph 2 on the same page*). Rocks, possibly even more than mountains, require a technique akin to sculpting. Photograph 3 on the same page shows the artist, having applied basic horizontal strokes and then white clay to his rock, delicately carving the final lines on the *keto*.

The technique employed when making a rock that has split in two is illustrated in Photographs 4-6. Never use two lumps of *keto* for this purpose; use one lump, make your rock, and then cut through it. The result is infinitely more natural.

68

Chapter 5   WATER, ITS SURFACE AND SHAPE

To recapitulate, the making of bodies of water usually involves the use of sand, with which the beginner is advised to familiarize himself. I shall here repeat the general rules, along with a few helpful details.

GENERAL CONSIDERATIONS

As was stated in the chapter on materials, the surface of bodies of water—from seas to swamps—is often composed of what we call ordinary "sea sand" that has been dyed blue. A finer sand, called *mazuna*, is also used for this purpose. Obviously, it would be to the advantage of the bonkei artist to keep a stock of sand of varied fineness and color from which to choose when the occasion arises. Whenever he comes across sand that may eventually be useful he ought to collect some: in that way, he will never be without the particular sand that he considers most advantageous to his immediate purpose. It should be borne in mind that all the sand should be dry, and should have been passed through a sieve or strainer to remove lumps and also to ensure that the grains are of a relatively uniform size.

After the mountains, rocks, and hills have been made out of *keto* or some substitute, the sand should be spooned into the various bodies of water, spread smooth, and then made even smoother still with a wide, dry brush. Then, using a syringe, gently sprinkle water at the corners. Afterwards, to ensure a maximum of smoothness, the tray should be lifted and tilted gently back and forth. Once this operation is complete, keep one corner of the tray slightly lower than the others so that excess water may collect there. This is removed by means of the syringe. After the level of the sand has been made as smooth as possible, a little more fine "sea sand" may be sprinkled through a sieve.

Sand, incidentally, is not the only means available to the artist to denote the surface of bodies of water. *Keto* may also be used, or a mirror placed in the desired position. Experienced bonkei-makers have always preferred sand, however, and my advice to the beginner is to acquire proficiency in its use before experimenting with other methods.

Rivers, as we noted earlier, are often simulated by use of the finest sand, called *mazuna*, but ordinary sea sand may also be used instead. Different types of rivers may become part of a bonkei. Wide rivers, for example, usually have their source in the high mountains, while narrow rivers and tributaries of wide rivers flow from smaller mountains. Since the tributaries often flow through villages, they may be given more interest by the addition of water-gates or footbridges. The sources of springs are usually found under trees or between rocks: this is why we have recommended the use of such ornaments to mark the source. A spring without its source clearly delineated produces an unbalanced effect. In all cases, rivers should be narrow in the distance and widen as they approach the foreground; and in all cases, also, as I mentioned in a previous chapter, winding rivers are more interesting than straight ones.

Once a body of water has been created, the problem arises of giving it a sense of motion—for water is never absolutely still, even on the calmest day. Of course, if you are using a mirror to represent the surface of the water, you have no choice, but if, as is more customary, your medium is sand, then you have the problem of deciding whether the ripples in rivers, lakes, and seas are to be barely perceptible or whether they should grow into waves that break resoundingly against the shore.

Before examining in detail the various methods available to the artist for the suggestion of motion in water, let us look first at a few of the commonest types of waves. In the case of the sea, the waves may simply lap gently at the shore, making hardly a murmur; or they may roll in, hurling themselves against the shore; or they may crash violently against high cliffs. It is also important to remember that in stormy weather great waves may be found far out at sea; inasmuch as these are in constant, violent motion, they offer considerable scope to the imagination of the artist.

Lake surfaces are generally placid, save when a strong wind is blowing, and it is customary to simulate a lake surface by means of small, barely perceptible ripples of sand.

River waves offer more variety, ranging from the gentle motion of a small stream to the great waves at the mouth of a large river that eddy and flow, as well as to the violence of a narrow, steep, mountain stream whose water seems anxious to destroy its rocky confines.

TECHNIQUES OF MAKING SEA WAVES

In all these cases, close observation of nature is essential—as well as a knowledge of the tricks of the trade. Look, for example, at photographs 1–7 on pages 71–73. Here the intention of the artist is to depict a quiet seaside. The first photograph shows it after the artist has made the necessary preparations—spooning in the sand, smoothing it with a brush, and adding water. In addition, using a fine sieve, he has sprinkled fine blue sand where he wants to suggest the sea; then, with a coarse sieve, he has sprinkled larger grains of blue sand where the sea meets the land. He has chosen two small stones, sprinkled them with artificial moss, and carefully placed them on the beach.

In the second photograph he begins the intricate process of creating the series of waves that indicate where the sea meets the land. First he takes some of the white-colored sand that suggests waves and drops it, little by little, along the beach. This process, although it can be accomplished by means of a sieve, appears more natural when it is done by hand. It requires both skill and experience. This first row of waves is comparatively wide, but the sand itself is spread thinly.

In photograph 3, the artist is creating the second and third line of breakers. Waves in the first and second rows are seen to be receding, while those in the third row are rolling toward the land. Their crests, therefore, should be higher than those of the other two. Where the two rows of receding waves separate, the sand forms a mound, its size dependent on the height of the waves.

Other waves, as may be seen in photograph 4, separate as they approach the land. The bright-colored, diagonal line in the distance represents the kind of wave that is created when the wind blows one sea against another. Here the artist, depending on the kind of weather he wants to suggest, is free to make waves as strong or as weak as he likes, but is probably best advised to keep their form short and sharp.

Photograph 5 is a typical seascape, with the waves dashing against the beach. Here also the artist determines the strength of the waves, depending on the kind of wind he wants to

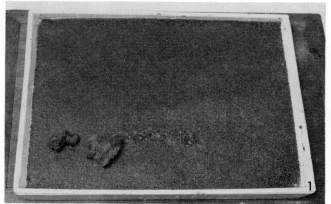

suggest as well as on the role he wants the rocks to play in the completed bonkei.

Should you want to depict high waves running in towards the beach, photograph 6 shows the best method of achieving this effect. Add more fine-grained sand at the points of separation of the waves; then sprinkle more wave sand. This method raises the base of the wave and consequently makes the wave itself seem higher. Now place the handle of your spatula in the base of the wave at several points and heave the sea sand up from under the base to achieve the desired turbulence.

Photograph 7 shows the completed process. In the fashioning of waves, the beginner must take care not to use too much sand, or he will fail altogether to give the illusion of waves. Also, only a few important points should be emphasized.

Freshwater waves are, of course, different in appearance from salt-sea waves, and, what is more, they themselves have considerable variety. They may be the turbulent waves of rapids, or the gentle lapping of a calm river at its water's edge. Other geographical factors, such as the width of the river, also affect the appearance of the waves. In addition, waves change their shape when they come into contact with stones or similar objects in the river, or when the water passes over submerged objects invisible to the eye. The bonkei artist, then, is obliged to study rivers of various types, as well as the same river at various places, if the goal of making a bonkei that is true to nature is to be achieved.

  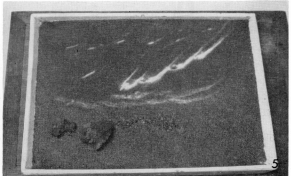

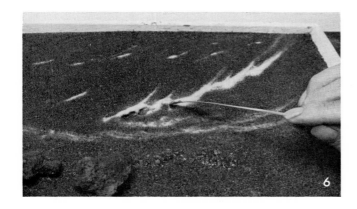

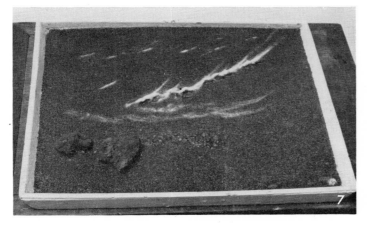

MAKING A RIVER AND WATERFALL

Let us look first at a river flowing from a waterfall (*photographs 1–4 on page 74*). In the first photograph, the mountain has already been modeled out of *keto*; then *mazuna* (river sand) is spread over the entire remainder of the surface of the tray, smoothed, and watered. Sea sand may be used for this purpose, but it will be found inferior to river sand. In a bonkei of this type, it is desirable to add a little more water than is customary in order to facilitate the making of waves.

Now drop wave sand from above the rock and incise vertical lines to suggest a swift-flowing waterfall. As the photograph suggests, this operation is best performed with the tips of the fingers.

In photograph 2, the fingertips are once again brought into play to suggest the foam at the foot of a turbulent waterfall. This is done by picking up the grains of wave sand and sprinkling them, one pinch after another, at the point where the water strikes the base of the falls. Gradually you will obtain the foamlike impression that is required.

Having achieved this essential illusion, begin the flow of water away from the base of the waterfall, as shown in photograph 3, by sprinkling the sand with your fingertips in a sweeping motion.

Photograph 4 shows the completed waterfall with the river flowing away from it. The current should, of course, seem strong and should be thinnest at the source, widening as the river progresses. Here, a boulder, placed centrally in the river, divides the foaming current into branches that spread out as the river broadens.

MAKING A WIDE RIVER

The making of another type of river is illustrated in photographs 1–4 on page 75 and 76. Here our problem is the depiction of the waves made by a wide river. Photograph 1 shows the tray with a layer of river sand on it (sea sand may be substituted if necessary) that has been smoothed and watered. The next step is to make the river bank, using some suitable ornament and sprinkling rough-grained sand around it in adequate quantities. To suggest the water of the current itself, fine-grained sea sand is generally used.

In Photograph 2, wave sand has been sprinkled next to the rough-grained sand to express the kind of waves that are usually found near the banks of rivers. The current should have an obvious curve to it, and there should be no question as to the direction of its flow from upriver.

The waves near both banks of the river should have continuity, as shown in photograph 3. They are made with exactly the same technique as that already outlined.

Photograph 4 shows the completed river, including the waves in the center, which are made with less sea sand than those at the banks since they do not have the same continuity. Furthermore, central waves may often strike against rocks in the water, in which case they form foaming white crests which must be depicted. The sand used to simulate a current may be colored either dark or light blue, suggesting either the depth or shallowness of the water. Where the artist desires to depict extremely deep water, a large quantity of very deep blue sand is used, whereas in shallow areas, such as at the banks, a pale blue sand is lightly sprinkled. Similar methods can be applied to narrow streams and the like, although, naturally, the final effect will be quite different.

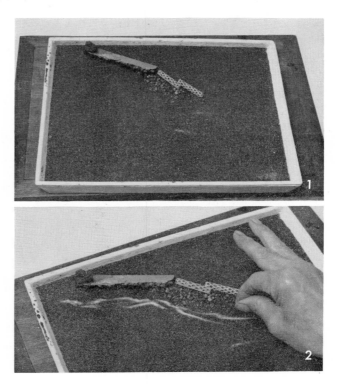

MAKING A LAKE

Waves are usually neither very common nor very violent on lakes and ponds, save when there is a gale blowing; but even on fairly calm days, faint ripples may be seen. Furthermore, bonkei scenes often depict a stream or a river flowing into a lake, and a slight disturbance of the water occurs at the point where the two meet. Photographs 1–4 on page 77 show the movement that may be suggested on a usually peaceful body of water like a lake.

Photograph 1 shows the initial stage. River sand by preference (or sea sand as a substitute) is poured over the surface of the tray. After it has been smoothed and watered, it is covered with fine-grained blue sand representing the water. Two or three stones are placed at the point where the river meets the lake, and between these stones the flow of the water is indicated. Use the method explained earlier for depicting waves in a stream flowing from the base of a waterfall, but make the waves both longer and more curved, and do not attempt to differentiate to the same extent between the thickness and thinness of various parts of the wave. Seek to achieve a subtler gradation. The waves of a stream flowing into a lake should be at least two and no more than five in number.

The waves on the lake itself, as shown in photograph 2, should be short and narrow, not very many in number, and with considerable space between them.

Unlike waves, of which there are only a few, ripples appear over the entire surface of the lake. This is shown in photographs 3 and 4.

On occasion, as I noted at the beginning of this chapter, a mirror may be used to suggest the surface of a body of water. This is particularly effective when the artist wants the surrounding landscape reflected in the water. An example might be a farmhouse standing directly on the banks of a lake. In front of the house, the red leaves of a maple, for instance, would be colorfully reflected in the mirror that forms the lake.

Chapter 6 SUBJECTS FOR BONKEI

I have already indicated certain of the rules that we in Japan consider fundamental to the making of a harmonious bonkei, but I should like here, before giving specific examples, to list all those that I consider essential. Many of them will be familiar to you—but a good teacher, I think, never hesitates to repeat a lesson!

Here, then, is my list of do's and don'ts for the beginner:

1. Whenever possible, indicate the source of a river (particularly if it flows straight across the tray).

2. Except in the case of distant mountains, do not attempt to make them rise abruptly from a plain, for this combination of forms would seem unnatural in mid-distant or foreground scenes. Where a mountain and a river appear in the same bonkei, one should harmonize with the other.

3. Avoid mountains, rocks, islands, and rivers that are similar in shape; two such features would be the maximum permissible in the same tray. Odd numbers are always preferable to even ones.

4. Do not have more than two parallel rivers or roads, and avoid making them run horizontally across the tray. To aid in giving the illusion of distance, rivers and roads should both widen as they approach the foreground.

5. The size of an ornament determines, to a certain extent, its position in the landscape—large houses, boats, and trees are placed in the foreground; smaller ones in the distance. Much the same is true of the leaves of trees: trees with broad leaves in the foreground, those with narrow ones in the distance.

6. The ebb and flow of the sea is ceaseless: waves come and go constantly at the shore, and even on the calmest days there are ripples farther out. Without this unceasing movement, a seascape would make an extremely dull bonkei.

7. The chief point about the average bonkei (landscape or seascape) is that it not only reflects but idealizes the beauty of nature. To do that, it must indicate the changing time of year, which is one of nature's greatest glories. For example, in the temperate zone (which is what chiefly concerns us) mountains are light green in spring, deep green in summer, red and yellow in autumn, snow-white in winter. A river in springtime is often in spate: it grows longer, wider, and

deeper, and takes more twists and turns; under the summer sun, it is likely to grow smaller and shallower; in autumn, the water itself seems clear and the river broad; while in winter, the river may freeze, in which case it is at its narrowest. Flowers also, of course, indicate the changing seasons, while their absence suggests the bareness of winter. 8. Common themes in Japanese bonkei are, as I have noted, mountains, hills, and cliffs, bodies of water, waterfalls, villages, and gardens. But, as I have also suggested, there is no need for the Westerner to confine himself to traditional Japanese themes. Once the techniques have been mastered, he is free to create any sort of bonkei.

The following are a few examples of traditional bonkei, with explanations of how to use the tools and materials. I do not recommend the beginner to slavishly copy them but rather, once he has fully understood the idea behind them, to go out and find a scene that has a personal appeal for him and that he can then attempt to transform into a bonkei expressing his own attitude towards the scene.

Mount Fuji and Lake Yamanaka

If a Japanese person were to take a mountain for his chief theme, Mount Fuji would, no doubt, be the first to come to mind—not only because it is the most famous mountain in Japan but also because it is, to a certain extent, the symbol of the country itself. Probably no other mountain in the world enjoys such wholehearted devotion.

But once having chosen Fuji-san, the Japanese bonkei artist is faced with the problem of fitting it into an acceptable composition. Simply to make a wide plain in the foreground with Fuji towering in the distance would be insufficient; lakes, rivers, or other manifestations of nature are vital if the composition is to be interesting. Fortunately, there are five lakes in the vicinity of the mountain, while the nearby Bay of Suruga opens onto the ocean. Thus, the artist who has chosen to depict Fuji has a wide choice of arrangements available to him. In this particular bonkei, I have used Lake Yamanaka (one of the five) as seen from the north. There still, of course, remains the problem of how to place both mountain and lake within the tray.

Since Fuji is the central object, I decided to put the mountain in the distance, just to the left of the center line, so that I could put Lake Yamanaka on the right. This arrangement, I confess, had the practical advantage of allowing me to create the waves of the lake with my right hand.

But since I considered it undesirable to have Mount Fuji rise too precipitously from the lake surface, I placed it to the right of center but allowed it to extend to the left edge of the tray. A hilly scene of this sort should be separated from Fuji itself by a short space.

The lake, which lies to the left of center, runs from the middle distance to the foreground. Trees—both large and small—are planted on the left side of the tray, where they serve as the dominant features of the foreground. The artist

79

is at liberty, naturally, to place houses, roads, walking figures, and the like, in the vicinity of the lake if he feels they will give added life to the scene. He might also place a fishing boat on the lake itself, at whatever point he considers would balance with his composition.

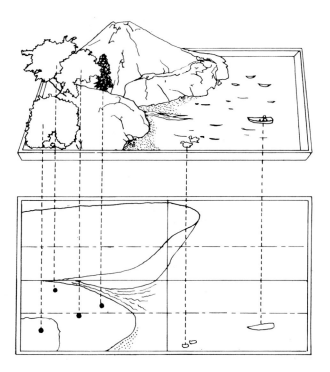

But we have been speaking in generalities, and the beginner, who has been experimenting with tools and materials but who has yet to create a completed bonkei, will want practical details. Here, then, is how to proceed. First place a lump of *keto* on the tray and divide it into several smaller pieces, roughly circular in shape, around two and a half inches in diameter. Making use of an *ate-ita*, pile the balls into a shape approximating that of the mountain (*photograph 1*).

Then cover the *keto* with a sheet of newspaper and begin the rough modelling of the mountain (*photograph 2*). Before beginning this operation, you will probably find it most convenient to cut two sheets of newspaper to the correct size, as shown in the photograph. (The purpose of the newspaper, incidentally, is merely to avoid soiling the hands.) Any sort of plastic wrapping, such as the kind used in the kitchen, may be substituted if it feels more comfortable.

Once you are satisfied that the *keto* has assumed a form roughly similar to that of Mount Fuji, remove the newspaper or other wrapping. You are now ready to begin the actual modelling, using the spatula in your right hand and the *ate-ita* (to hold the *keto* in position) in your left (*photograph 3*). As described earlier, you use the spatula to make folds in the mountain and also to push the *keto* upward to form the foothills. If you push with too much force, the angle of incline toward the valley will be too sharp. The actual folds are now made by pressing in the tip of the spatula

and making downward strokes (*diagram 1*). The summit of Mount Fuji, although it appears from a distance to come almost to a point, is in fact flat and triangular: this must be suggested. Mount Fuji, from a distance, also appears to be an almost perfect cone, but this is not true either, so the artist must take care not to make the angle of incline too sharp. Behind the mountain, leave a space about twice the width of the spatula (*diagram 2*) which can be used for drainage when adding water, as must regularly be done to keep the *keto* from cracking and losing its shape.

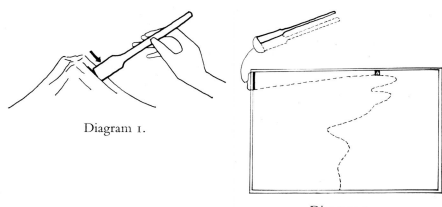

Diagram 1.

Diagram 2.

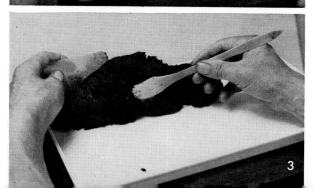

Then, once again using techniques already described, add white clay, by means of the spatula, to emphasize the folds of the mountain (*photograph 4*). At the same time, create the hilly region in the middle distance; should you find the *keto* insufficient, you may now take a fresh supply.

In photograph 5, the mountain, as well as the hills in front of it, are shown with the white clay process completed.

The hills at the shore of the lake in the left foreground are made by the same method as the mountain itself. That is to say, two balls of *keto* are covered with paper, roughly molded, and then, with the paper removed, finished with the spatula and the *ate-ita* (*photograph 6*). The artist must be careful not to create a deep valley and must be sure that the mountain, its foothills, and the hills beyond, all blend naturally together.

Photograph 7 shows the planting of trees in the foreground hills. These are trees that have been grown in small bonsai trays, and the process of replanting them is roughly as follows: water is poured into the bonsai tray, after which the trees are carefully uprooted. The roots are then wrapped in newspaper and soaked in water until any soil still clinging to them is loosened. Once that has been removed, the roots are rewrapped in moistened newspaper and planted in the *keto* (*see Chapter 8*).

Since this process of planting in *keto* is done only on the right side of the hill, the newspaper-wrapped roots on the left side are exposed to view. To conceal these, use some

82

4

5

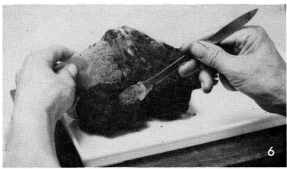

6

7

moss to which the soil still adheres and which has been thoroughly watered. After planting the moss with some pincers (*photograph 8*), the areas around the moss are pressed in firmly with the spatula. At the same time, the *keto* into which the trees have been planted is patted into place and touched up with white clay (*photograph 8*).

The next step is to add a solution of colcothar (*benigara*) to both the mountain and the hills in the middle distance and foreground. Although this is done by means of a brush, the technique used is not that of painting but is one peculiar to bonkei. The solution is brushed onto the summit and allowed to trickle down the slopes (*photograph 9*). The solution will not adhere to plain *keto*, only to areas where white clay has been used.

Now (*photograph 10*) add the finishing touches by brushing on a solution of yellow powder (*tonoko*), avoiding areas where the colcothar is thick, and finally add the shadows with a verdigris solution. The three solutions combine with the dark *keto* and the white clay to make the mountains slopes seem alive with trees.

Once the solutions have blended, you will be able to decide where to sprinkle artificial green moss, since your aim is to avoid places where the solutions have combined to resemble bare rocks. Also, with a mountain as high as Fuji, you should not sprinkle moss above the timber line. The technique used (*photograph 11*) is to hold the sieve in the right hand and lightly tap the handle with the right forefinger.

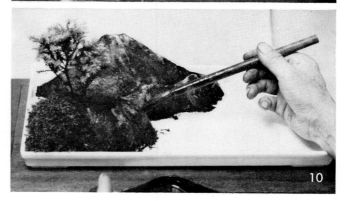

After you have completed the green moss operation, add artificial yellow moss to suggest areas that are bathed in sunlight, and artificial dark green moss for areas that receive little or no sun. These mosses are best sprinkled by hand (*photograph 12*).

In the center of the hilly area in the middle distance, sprinkle coarse brown sand in the form of a road, to give the impression that the hills can be crossed (*photograph 13*).

Plant three small artificial trees (one cedar and two pines) between the bonsai tree and the mountain (*photograph 14*). By contrasting with the larger natural tree in the foreground, these help create the essential illusion of distance.

Similar small artificial trees may be used in other areas of the middle distance, as well as on the foothills of Mount Fuji, to denote distant forests (*photograph 15*).

Now, to create the lake, sprinkle blue sand through a

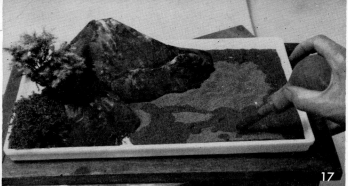

coarse sieve into the remaining space: the sand should be about one-half the depth of the tray (*photograph 16*).

After levelling the sand with your spatula or with a wide, dry brush, add water, using a syringe, to make the surface still smoother (*photograph 17 and diagram 3*).

If necessary, tilt the tray slightly back and forth so that the sand is thoroughly saturated (*photograph 18*). Then, with a sieve, sprinkle sea sand in the hollows of the moist sand.

Tilt the tray once again so that excess water collects in the hollow behind Mount Fuji (*see diagram 4*); remove this excess water with the syringe (*see diagram 5*).

With your fingertips (*photograph 19*), sprinkle medium-grained beach sand along the base of the hills in the foreground.

Suggest a stream flowing into the lake from behind the hills in the foreground by dropping wave sand little by little

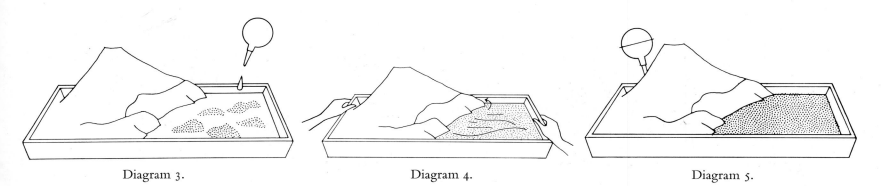

Diagram 3.   Diagram 4.   Diagram 5.

between thumb and forefinger (*photograph 20*). The waves should grow less imposing as they recede.

Put a fishing boat on the surface of the lake, on the right side, to balance the mountain and hills on the left. The completed bonkei is shown in photograph 21.

Lighthouse on a Cliff

Since the usual purpose of a lighthouse is both to guide and to warn ships at sea, the bonkei artist who desires to incorporate one in his composition has in reality but two choices: he may build it either on a cliff or promontory standing high above the sea or on a high rock protruding from the sea itself. Both sea and lighthouse are essential elements in such a composition: they must, therefore, be balanced.

Obviously, one of the ways to make the sea as eye-catching as the lofty lighthouse is through the use of waves, and since it is easier to create waves with the right hand, we should place the sea to the right of center in a wide space that includes both far distant, middle distant, and foreground areas. We then have no choice but to place the cliff with its lighthouse on the left side of the tray, beginning virtually at the left edge. Since it must be strongly emphasized, we put the cliff itself in the middle distance, with the approaches to the cliff in the foreground. In order to attain further balance in the composition, boats at sea and protruding rocks should be equated with fishermen's huts on the cliff and drying nets. This is the basis of our composition; it now remains for us to see how to transform it into a finished bonkei.

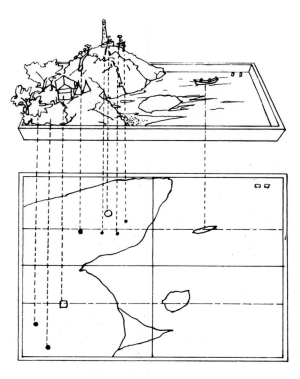

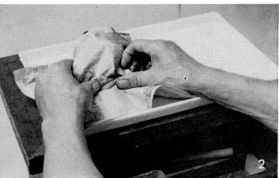

First, we place several balls of *keto*, one on top of the other, in the position we have chosen for the cliff (*photograph 1*). Only after the shape and size of the cliff and the land surrounding it have become clear in our mind can we arrange the balls of *keto* in a suitable fashion for further work.

We then cover them, following the familiar system, with paper (*photograph 2*) and mold them roughly into the shape of both cliff and lower land, taking care to separate the cliff which dominates the middle distance from the land in the foreground. In fact, it is probably advisable to mold the two separately.

The rough shapes, after the paper has been removed, are shown in photograph 3.

Now, using a spatula in one hand and an *ate-ita* in the other, begin to give the *keto* a form closer to the one finally envisaged (*photograph 4*). The *keto* that you have cut away with your spatula can be used, as you will see later, to form an island in the bay and to bring the two elements of sea and land into closer harmony.

Still making use of spatula and *ate-ita*, mold the shapes still further (*photograph 5*), seeking always to achieve the ideal balance that is the essence of Japanese bonkei. Note that the right side of the cliff, where it meets the lower land, is very steep. As before, make folds in both cliff and land with white clay using the point of your spatula, placing particular emphasis on the side of the cliff that plunges vertically into the sea.

4

5

6

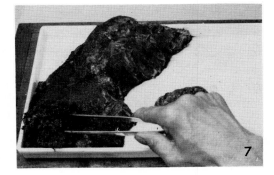

7

As described in the previous bonkei, paint the land, cliff, and island with solutions of colcothar, *tonoko*, and verdigris in that order (*photograph 6*). Then sprinkle artificial moss, again using yellow for particularly sunlit areas and dark green for shaded areas. The land in the left foreground must be kept free of both paint and moss, for it is here that the fisherman's house is to stand. All you need do is make sure that the land is level.

Moisten natural moss—tall moss for bushes, shorter moss for grass—and, using pincers, plant it in the left foreground in front of the area where you are going to place the house (*photograph 7*).

Now imbed the house firmly behind the moss and level the space around it with your spatula so that it stands squarely (*photograph 8*).

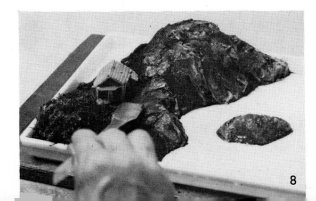

8

  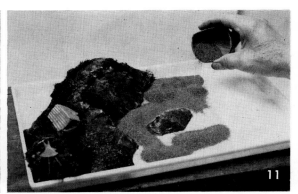

Plant short moss towards the back of the cliff and anywhere else in that area where you wish to give the impression of a distant forest. Here, once again, you use your pincers (*photograph 9*).

Sprinkle beach sand from the front of the house along the top of the cliff (*photograph 10*) to indicate the sea encroaching upon the land. Drape fishing nets to dry over the moss in the left foreground.

Sprinkle blue sand over the remaining space to a depth of about one-half that of the tray. Less sand (merely enough to cover the bottom of the tray) would be sufficient, but a thicker layer of sand makes the bonkei last longer (*photograph 11*). Make the sand as smooth as possible with a brush and then water, using the methods previously described.

You will probably be able to find a suitable lighthouse at a nearby toy shop, but if you are unable to, or if you prefer to make your own one, simply cut a sheet of thick white paper into the desired shape (*as shown in photograph 12*) and paint in the windows. If you use a simple sheet of paper, you will find it advisable to back it with something stiff, like a small piece of wood or bamboo, to keep it from bending.

Photograph 13 shows the lighthouse being placed in position on top of the cliff in the middle distance.

In photograph 14, the position of the fishing nets is being changed to the right of the house as the artist, after seeing the house and lighthouse in place, found their former position unsatisfactory.

90

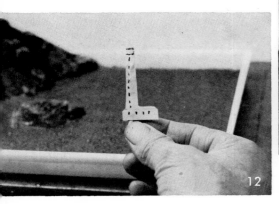

He then replaces some of the moss with small trees (*photograph 15*).

As we have noted before, in order to achieve the maximum of balance we use trees with small leaves in the distance, while those with broad leaves are placed in the foreground. The trees are rootless and are simply pressed into the damp moss and the *keto* (*photograph 16*).

Plant artificial pines on the topmost ridge of the cliff in the middle distance, as well as behind the house and in front of the lighthouse (*photograph 17*). The purpose of these pines is to give a feeling of vitality and contrast to the bonkei.

At the foot of the cliff, around the water's edge, sprinkle small and medium-sized grains of sand, and top them off with larger grains (*photograph 18*).

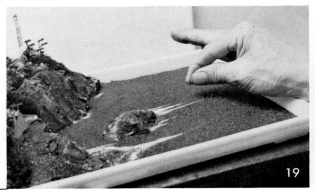

Make high waves (using wave sand) near the edge of the cliff and around the island (*photograph 19*).

Continue the wave-making process by adding somewhat smaller waves under the cliff in the middle distance as well as on the surface of the sea (*photograph 20*). Once again you will probably have recourse to a toy shop to find the kind and size of fishing boat most suitable for the composition, although you may of course prefer to construct your own out of thin strips of wood painted to harmonize with the rest of the bonkei. In any case, the best place for it, as shown in the photograph, is towards the far distance.

Cut out a couple of strips of thick white paper (to suggest the white masts of sailing boats) and place them carefully with pincers against the inner right side of the tray in the sea sand (*photograph 21*). They help contribute towards a feeling of depth.

The completed bonkei—"Lighthouse on a Cliff"—is shown in photograph 22.

21

22

A River in a Mountain Gorge

As we noted earlier, bonkei recognizes a number of different types of rivers that may be incorporated into, or become the central theme of, a traditional composition. Here, we have chosen to depict a river of medium width which is the tributary of a larger river. It is wide enough for the use of both rafts and bridges, which become essential elements in the composition; and because the traditional bonkei artist always likes to suggest, if not to pinpoint, the source of a river, mountains are used to tell us that the river has come tumbling down a gorge before it widens in the plain. As always, we do our best to give the river a bend or two to make the composition more interesting.

In this bonkei, the mountains are situated both on the left half of the tray, the lowest ones in the foreground, and on the other side of the gorge, permitting them to rise to high peaks in the far distance. To assist us in achieving a more exciting bonkei, we make use of village houses, a suspension bridge, and baskets of stones collected to reinforce the riverbanks. Naturally, our mountains require isolated trees as well as forests and even, in this case, torrents to contribute to the total effect we are trying to achieve. The right half of the tray is given over to a wide open space where the tributary joins the larger river. Let us now examine in detail the means by which we create this particular bonkei.

93

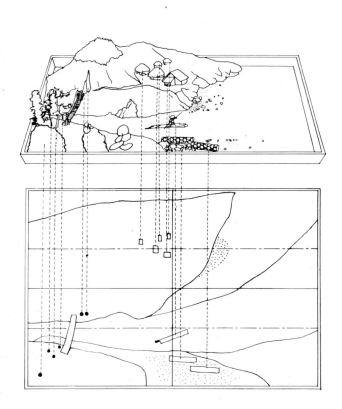

We begin work with the mountains that are to occupy the middle and far distant scenes on the left side of the tray slightly behind the center line. Using the methods with which we are now familiar, we place several lumps of *keto* on the tray, cover them with paper, and model them roughly into the desired forms. Then, after removing the paper (*photograph 1*), we begin to develop the initially rough forms using spatula and *ate-ita*. We must remember that the back of the mountain is perpendicular.

We must also bear in mind that the tallest mountain should lie fairly far to the left in the middle distance and should descend gradually to the distant range. Anticipating the finished bonkei, create a hollow in the center of the middle distant range, which is where the houses of a tiny mountain village will eventually stand. Then form a hilly area on

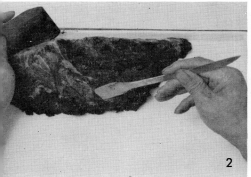

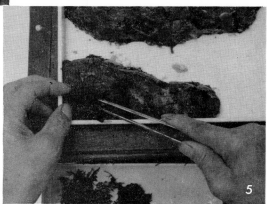

the left-hand side of the mountain in the middle distance so that it may be related to the smaller mountain in the foreground. Apply white clay with your spatula to create folds in the mountain surface and shadows in the valleys (*photograph 2*).

Place another ball or two of *keto* in the front left corner of the tray and mold the mountains that will comprise the left foreground, leaving space between them and the larger mountains in the middle distance (*photograph 3*).

As you have done before, take your brush and apply color to the mountains, using the familiar solutions of colcothar, *tonoko*, and verdigris (*photograph 4*).

On the mountains in the foreground, plant tall moss as well as broad-bladed grass (*photograph 5*). This more or less completes the scene in the immediate foreground.

Now plant short moss on the hilly areas and on the summits of the mountain range in the far distance to denote forests (*photograph 6*).

Using your sieve with a handle, as shown in photograph 7, sprinkle artificial green moss but avoid the space where you intend to create your little mountain village.

In that particular area, sprinkle sand as a base for a road (*photograph 8*).

With the handle of your spatula, make a road winding its way from the village up the slopes of the mountain in the middle distance (*photograph 9*).

Using a small brush, paint the road with a solution of *tonoko* (*photograph 10*).

Should the effect seem meager, add more *tonoko* to the road with the tip of the handle of your spatula (*photograph 11*).

96

Sprinkle yellow green moss on the ridges of the mountains in the middle distance to give the effect of sprouting vegetation (*photograph 12*).

Fill the empty area of the tray with *mazuna* (*photograph 13*) and level it off, as you have done before, with brush and water, draining off any excess. To denote rivers and lakes, *mazuna* may be used in place of sea sand (*photograph 13*).

Now sprinkle beach sand on the right-hand area to create a river bed (*photograph 14*). The banks of the river follow the curves of the mountains in the foreground and middle distance through which the river flows. Coarse-grained beach sand is used for places nearest the land and finer sand in the more immediate neighborhood of the river.

Fill the space between the mountains with blue sand, sprinkled through a sieve as shown in photograph 15, to denote the widening river as it flows toward the plain.

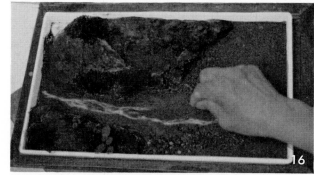

 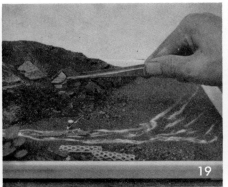 

18 19 20

21

Using your pincers, carefully place whatever ornaments you have at hand (or care to make) that seem well suited to the scene. In our completed bonkei, we have used, apart from the village itself which is essential, a suspension bridge, a man poling a raft, and some baskets of stones (*photograph 17*).

If you use a suspension bridge, plant artificial trees on both sides of it (*photograph 18*).

Place the village houses with extreme care so as not to disrupt the harmony of the entire composition (*photograph 19*). Plant a couple of artificial pine trees behind the village.

As a final touch, place small pieces of living moss in *keto* on top of the mountains in the far distance to suggest forests (*photograph 20*).

The completed bonkei is shown in photograph 21.

Teahouse in a Garden

Our prime purpose in this bonkei is to create a garden, but experience has taught us that a garden alone is inadequate: it lacks a chief point of interest, a focus to give it drama. So we must decide whether to make that point of interest a pond, an elaborate flower-bed, a house of some kind, or perhaps a background of eye-catching mountains. In this particular case, we have chosen that typically Japanese construction—the teahouse, which is no more that than what it claims to be, a small and unpretentious shelter where people repair to drink green tea in meditative silence or in lofty conversation, and to admire both the simple beauty of the tea implements and the dexterity with which the hostess (or the host) uses them. To give additional interest to the composition, we have included three ladies on their way to the teahouse, and because the Japanese always insist on knowing the season, we have clearly indicated that the time of year is spring.

Since we have decided to leave out the more dramatic manifestations of nature such as lakes and high mountains, the entire surface of the tray will be occupied by the garden. Our first consideration, then, is the placing of the teahouse. If we were to build it in the central foreground, it would not only hide most of the rest of the garden from view, but it would also make one of the dullest compositions imaginable. We will, therefore, place it in the background, a little off-center—in this case, slightly to the right. To balance it, a small hill of approximately equivalent size will lie on the left-hand side of the tray, in front of which we will lay a path for our human figures to follow on their way to the teahouse. We will, of course, make use of the trees and flowers appropriate to a garden in springtime and also enhance the composition by adding a small pond in the foreground, where a couple of ducks, or other waterfowl, have settled.

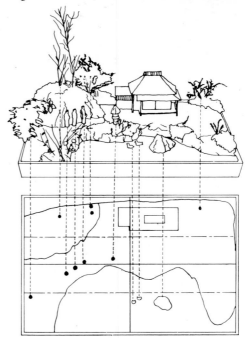

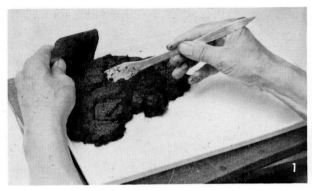  

The first step, as usual, is to take a few balls of *keto*, perhaps four or five, and place them on the left side of the tray, where they are covered with paper, modelled into a rough shape, then molded more finely with spatula and *ate-ita* (*photograph 1*). It is important to remember to leave areas on the hill where trees may be planted.

Remove a tree from its bonsai tray, wrap its roots in newspaper, and plant it strategically on the hill (*photograph 2*); its exact location is, of course, a matter you can decide only on the basis of your total composition.

Pat *keto* firmly around the roots of the tree; this will somewhat increase the height of the hill (*photograph 3*).

Continue working with spatula and *ate-ita* to achieve the desired form of the hill (*photograph 4*), adding more *keto* should that prove necessary to accomplish your purpose.

Smooth out a thin layer of *keto* in the foreground in front of the hill and plant it with grass (*photograph 5*).

Do the same on the right side, leaving a blank area that will eventually serve as the pond and extending the *keto* into the distance but leaving it flat, for it is there that you will place the house. As always, leave a thin, undecorated strip at the back of the tray that will serve as drainage for excess water (*photograph 6*).

In photograph 7 the artist is seen adding white-clay solution with the tip of his spatula to both the hill and the low surrounding ground.

Plant some bonsai cedars (their roots, as usual, wrapped in paper) near the hill (*photograph 8*).

Pack *keto* around the roots of the newly planted trees and cover the *keto* with moss, using your pincers (*photograph 9*).

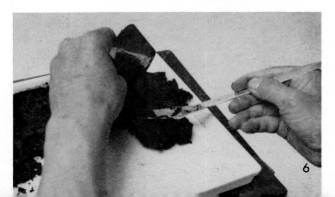

Level the distant area with your spatula until it is absolutely smooth, then place your teahouse with the utmost care; it is, after all, the chief element around which the composition revolves. It is very likely that, unless you are living in Japan and have access to a bonkei supply shop, you will have to construct your own teahouse. Its extreme simplicity renders the job fairly easy—save, perhaps, for the thatched roof (for which you may decide to use the bristles of a broom). In any case, you will need ingenuity and patience and will probably not succeed in constructing a satisfactory thatched roof the first time you try. But you will find the challenge an exciting one—and success extremely satisfying. Once the house has been built and put in place, level off the space in front of it with your spatula (*photograph 10*).

Now add a bit of *keto* just to the left of the house, in the middle distance, to serve as a kind of promontory for the pond, which will eventually occupy much of the foreground. Plant this *keto* with grass and moss (*photograph 11*).

Behind the promontory, place a typical Japanese stone lantern (which may, of course, be made of paper, papier-mâché, pottery, or any substance you consider suitable). The placing of it is shown in photograph 12.

Using pincers, plant moss in the hollow on the right side of the pond, moistening it with water (*photograph 13*).

Plant branches of small-leaved trees in the right background: these are intended to represent real trees (*photograph 14*).

The same applies to photograph 15, where moss has been

planted on the promontory on the right and branches pressed into the moss to simulate trees.

To help balance the scene, trees are also planted on the lower part of the hill at the left side of the tray—those with broad leaves in front, those with smaller leaves at the rear (*photograph 16*).

Using pincers, plant natural moss on various areas of the slopes of the hill (*photograph 17*).

With your brush, paint the surface of the hill (where no moss has been planted) and the rocky banks of the pond with the three familiar solutions (*photograph 18*). It goes without saying that the brush must be washed after every use so as not to muddy the pigments; another cardinal rule is never to paint level ground.

Place in the pond area a rock large enough to rise gracefully over the sand that will eventually represent the water of the pond (*photograph 19*).

Using a sieve with a handle, sprinkle green moss from the lower slopes of the hill across the level ground to the edge of the pond (*photograph 20*).

With the same sieve, sprinkle sand for the path leading from the middle of the left edge of the tray up to the teahouse (*photograph 21*). If you vary the size of the grains,

using the coarsest ones where the path is nearest the foreground, you will attain a sharper sense of distance.

To help denote the season of the year, sprinkle yellow green sand beside the road up to the edge of the pond (*photograph 22*).

Sprinkle sea sand in the space you have left vacant for the pond (*photograph 23*). Level it off with a brush, add water, and shake the tray slightly to ensure that the sand is as smooth as possible. Remove excess water with a syringe.

Over this, sprinkle colored sand through a wide-meshed sieve to denote the surface of the pond (*photograph 24*).

Carefully place two or three waterfowl near the rock in the pond; you should have no trouble finding miniatures of a suitable size at a toy shop, although you may want to change their coloring slightly to ensure that they become an integral part of the garden (*photograph 25*). Once the fowl are in place, add small ripples nearby to suggest they are in motion.

As with the waterfowl, you should have little or no difficulty finding kimono-clad Japanese dolls to serve as the human figures making their way towards the teahouse. Or you should be able to make your own figures easily enough if you prefer to use kimono material of your own choosing. Place the figures carefully, with an eye to the entire scene (*photograph 26*).

The completed bonkei is shown in photograph 27.

A Waterfall, with Mountain Stream and Lake

Japan, a mountainous country with an adundance of water, is famous for its waterfalls: a list of those the Japanese make special visits to would be too long for the pages of this book, which is not, after all, a guide to the topography of Japan but rather a guide to the bonkei that may be derived from its famous scenes, and by extension, from the equally famous and dramatic scenes of other countries of the world. As always, our aim is not to copy a waterfall exactly, but to use it as a point of reference for a waterfall of our own creation. In this particular bonkei, the water drops a great distance from a tall mountain, and the scene is further enhanced by a mountain lake and stream.

Here, as before, our problem is how to arrange the elements of the composition so as to achieve a harmonious bonkei that best expresses the theme uppermost in our minds. We balance the elements by putting the waterfall itself on the left-hand side of the tray and the stream which it forms on the right. The mountain and waterfall occupy the middle distance, and since the waterfall is the "eye-catcher" of the scene, the mountain must be high enough to produce an imposing fall of water. The lake fills the distant scene, and the gushing stream the foreground. Let us see how it works in practice.

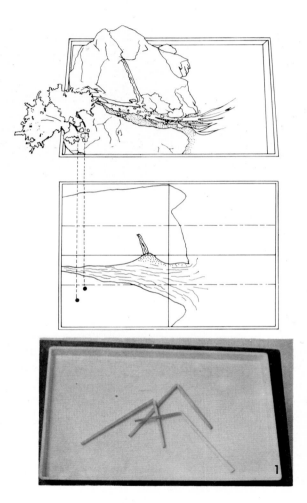

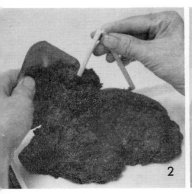

Because we want to make the mountain as high as is practicable, and because *keto* is soft and likely to bend in one direction or another if built to too great a height, we begin by making a sturdy framework to support the mountain. (In Japan, we would use chopsticks, which are available everywhere, but there is no reason why any other sort of thin stick should not serve equally well—or, for that matter, stiff lengths of wire.) This preliminary framework may be seen in photograph 1.

In building the mountain itself, do not be niggardly with the *keto*: bear in mind that this is to be an extremely tall mountain, with a high, dramatic waterfall. Therefore, pile the balls of *keto* up until you feel your mountain is grand enough, then cover it, as always, with paper and do your preliminary modelling. After you have removed the paper, stick the two halves of a chopstick (or some similar supports) through the top of the mountain to help keep it rigid (*photograph 2*).

Two additional pieces of broken wood (or bent wire) should now be inserted into the sides (*photograph 3*).

Using your spatula and *ate-ita*, and working up from the bottom, make sure that all supports are covered by *keto* (*photograph 4*).

Add more *keto* to the back of the summit and pat it firmly into place so that the mountain stands firm and solid; the back should be perpendicular, rather like a precipitous cliff, and behind it there should be a thin runnel for drainage of water (*photograph 5*).

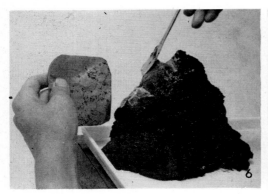

Having completed your work with the *keto*, add folds of white clay to the summit with the sharp edge of your spatula (*photograph 6*): your aim in this operation is to make the emergence of a high waterfall seem natural.

After finishing work on the lower part of the mountain in the middle scene, turn your attention to the still lower, rocky hill in the left foreground. One of the essentials for this hill is a natural (bonsai) tree, whose roots are moistened and wrapped in newspaper before being planted in the *keto* (*photograph 7*).

Once you are satisfied with the location of the tree, add the finishing touches to the small hill itself (*photograph 8*).

Now add more *keto* to establish a connection between the mountain in the middle distance and the hill in the foreground, as well as to make the lower areas of both more substantial (*photograph 9*). Still more *keto* may be added to join these lower areas; at the same time take care to leave an indentation for the waterfall (*photograph 10*).

Holding your spatula vertically, carve out a hollow for the waterfall (*photograph 11*).

The three colored solutions with which you are by now familiar are applied to the rocky mountain in the middle distance as far as the summit (*photograph 12*) and also to the rocky hill in the foreground.

Plant tall moss around the foot of the tree on the mountain in the foreground (*photograph 13*).

Short moss may now be planted on the sides and summit of the foreground mountain, as well as in the region near the source of the waterfall (*photograph 14*). The purpose of this short moss is to contribute a sense of distance.

Photograph 15 shows dark green moss being sprinkled lightly over the entire scene to denote grass and trees. The moss is sprinkled by tapping the handle of the sieve lightly with the forefinger.

With your fingertips, sprinkle dark green moss wherever you would like to suggest a forest (*photograph 16*). In order to reach less accessible areas on the mountain, the tray should be slightly tilted.

As a contrast, sprinkle yellow green moss on sunlit areas (*photograph 17*); this also serves to create a sense of distance. Then sprinkle road sand lightly with your fingertips on the foreground mountain.

In the right-hand half of the tray, sprinkle sea sand and smooth it with a brush, then pour in water, level it, and remove excess water. Then with your sieve sprinkle blue sand to complete the surface of the lake (*photograph 18*).

There follows a procedure that, while not especially difficult, is obviously essential to the bonkei as a whole. With a fine brush and white poster color, paint in the waterfall around which the whole scene revolves (*photograph 19*). To give a three-dimensional effect to the waterfall, drop wave sand directly from above.

Sprinkle beach sand from the base of the waterfall down to where the water enters the lake (*photograph 20*).

Use wave sand to create a sense of motion in this same stretch of water (*photograph 21*). The same sand may be used to give the illusion of waves on the upper reaches of the river at left, and also in the river as it plunges into the lake.

Plant artificial pines around the source of the waterfall (*photograph 22*).

Photograph 23 shows the completed bonkei after the addition of two more artificial pines and a cedar.

22

23

FARMHOUSES WITH WATER-GATE

In Japan, a farmhouse usually stands amid the farmer's field of growing grain, but this would probably make for a rather dull bonkei, so I have chosen instead to depict two farmhouses in a lush thicket watered by a stream, with a water-gate of the kind that farmers use. The two cottages stand just to right and left of center, towards the back of the tray. The middle scene contains a field of flowering rape, with the water-gate on the left. In the foreground flows the stream itself, crossed by two earthwork bridges. Behind the houses stand artificial trees, with a watchtower on the right; trees that are intended to serve as a windbreak are planted between the far distant and middle distant areas on the left-hand side of the tray. An artificial cherry tree is placed on the right to give an added touch to the scene.

As the reader will have observed, this particular bonkei requires a large number of ornaments (*shown in photograph 1, page 112*). From left to right, in the back row, they include a water-gate and the two farmhouses; in the front row, a watchtower, a wooden barrier to prevent the riverbank from collapsing, and the two earthwork bridges mentioned earlier. The tiny figures in the center are a farmer and his workhorse.

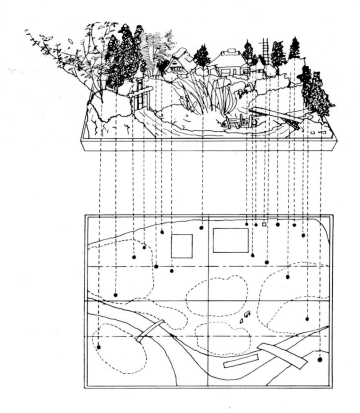

To begin work on the bonkei, place *keto* on the tray, cover it with newspaper, and model it to form the level ground that occupies most of the composition. The *keto* should be laid rather thickly since it will have to sustain not only the other ornaments and trees but also the water-gate (*photograph 2*).

Spread the *keto* on the right side of the tray and plant living trees in the clear space on the left (*photograph 3*).

Now add more *keto* to the left foreground, forming a small mound, while firmly patting *keto* around the roots of the trees. Leave sufficient space (of an attractive shape) in the right foreground for the river to flow across the bonkei (*photograph 4*). Place the water-gate at the point that seems most natural to you, and behind it, towards the right, plant living trees.

Plant tall grass towards the edge of the empty space where the river will be, and place the barrier nearby to suggest the proximity of the water. Now, in the right foreground, at the very corner, model a small bit of land and carefully lay one of the earthwork bridges over it (*photograph 5*).

Put the two houses in place as shown in photograph 6.

Spread natural moss around the roots of the trees and by the banks of the stream. Paint the cliffs that form the banks of the stream with the three solutions you are now familiar with; inasmuch as there are no mountains in this bonkei, the use of the colored solutions is here limited to the rocky banks of the stream (*photograph 7*).

Plant natural moss in the *keto* in front of the houses and then sprinkle yellow artificial moss to simulate the field of rape flowers (*photograph 8*). Or you may prefer to use red moss for azaleas, green moss for a tea field, or mixed yellow and red moss to represent maple trees.

To obtain the necessary sense of distance, plant large artificial trees on the left-hand side of the tray and small trees behind the houses (*photograph 9*).

Additional large artificial trees are placed in the right foreground, and cherry trees to the right of the houses. Using your pincers, carefully place the watchtower behind the trees (its purpose is to serve as a lookout for possible forest fires). These are all shown in place in photograph 10.

Fill in the river with blue sand (sea or river sand), smooth it as usual, and moisten it (*photograph 11*).

Create ripples in the stream, using wave sand (*photograph 12*). Photograph 13 shows the completed bonkei.

11

12

13

Chapter 7 TYPES OF BONKEI

The usual horizontal tray landscape is, as I mentioned earlier in this book, by no means the only method of expression the bonkei artist may resort to. I should now like to describe the various kinds of bonkei in general use, and the methods of construction that differentiate them from the horizontal tray we have been discussing. Its obvious converse is, of course, the vertical bonkei, of which there are several variations and most of which, like the horizontal bonkei, tend to have *keto* as their primary material. So also does the more elaborate "table bonkei," used particularly as a table decoration for a party or for some other special occasion. The exception to all of these is the dry bonkei, which uses exclusively artificial materials, and which, as a consequence, endures for a much longer time. Dry materials are generally used for framed bonkei.

VERTICAL BONKEI

The ordinary vertical bonkei may be used in three quite different ways: 1. supported by a stand; 2. hanging on a wall in its tray; or 3. framed.

It is customary in making a vertical bonkei to lean the tray at an angle so that the artist will have a clearer conception of his finished composition. As shown in the photograph on the opposite page, the artist very often makes use of a kind of easel not unlike that used in painting; the work angle is generally about sixty degrees. Although the easel is not essential, as the artist may simply lean his tray against a wall, he will probably find it a useful piece of equipment if he plans to do much vertical bonkei.

Since the work is done at an angle, it obviously differs both in technique and in material from the making of horizontal bonkei. A further difference is that the artist is free to make use of ideas that would not be practical in flat bonkei, such as including the sun or moon in his work. What is more, in a vertical bonkei he may increase the three-dimensionality of mountains or waterfalls without distorting the composition as a whole. Since *keto* adheres to the tray, it offers no special problem; but sand does not adhere, and if it is being used to denote the sky, it must first be colored and then mixed with some adhesive to keep it in place.

A mountain waterfall is well expressed in this typical framed bonkei.

Easel for a standing bonkei. It is constructed in the form of a tripod.

HANGING BONKEI

Hanging bonkei—as opposed to standing bonkei—is probably a late development in the history of the art, and came into being only after hanging vases first began to be used for ikebana. Hanging flower vases of almost any shape may be employed, but the area they offer is usually very limited, so it is practically impossible to create a grandiose landscape of the kind we have become familiar with in flat bonkei. And even if it were, the completed landscape would probably not be very pleasing to the eye. I recall that I once created a hanging bonkei in a round bowl to decorate a Japanese restaurant —only to discover, once it was done, that it looked better standing than hanging.

I would not, however, like to discourage the beginner from attempting a hanging bonkei. It can be an exciting experience, with highly satisfactory results. My only words of caution are that it is not really in the mainstream of bonkei as an art and so is best limited to flowers and miniature trees.

FRAMED BONKEI

This has certain similarities to the standing and even the hanging bonkei. Like the standing bonkei, it may use the sky as a background, but whereas the standing bonkei is created in an easel and may remain displayed in that same easel its entire lifetime (a period limited by the life of the *keto*), the framed bonkei is deliberately made of artificial material, and the question of "dying" does not arise. Once finished, it is

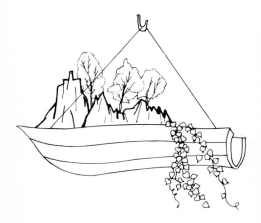

An example of hanging bonkei.

A framed dry bonkei, in which the basic material is papier-mâché mixed with white clay. Here, the Imperial Palace in Tokyo is represented with the famous Double Bridge in the foreground.

Dry bonkei: the basic material is newsprint and white clay, and the flowers and trees are artificial.

framed and hung on the wall, and since a strong adhesive is used in its making, it may even be tilted forward without danger of pieces of it coming loose and falling off.

THE BASIC MATERIAL OF DRY BONKEI

It was about fifteen years ago that I appeared on a television program in Tokyo demonstrating the making of a bonkei. During the course of the program, the announcer remarked that the bonkei was so lovely it was a pity it could not be preserved indefinitely. "It seldom lasts more than a month,"

I replied, but after the program I began to ponder the question of using, instead of *keto*, easily obtainable artificial materials that could be preserved much longer. Having heard that the late Mr. Kansui Koyama, master of the Shinsen School, had spent long years of study attempting to perfect the use of newsprint as a suitable material for a dry bonkei, I determined to take up where he left off. It was in this way that I hit upon the idea of combining newsprint with white clay and charcoal.

But first I should like to describe the method that Mr.

118

Koyama evolved, for it forms the basis of my own method. His system was to take some fifty newspaper sheets, tear each in two, and crumple each half into a ball which he would then drop into a large pot of boiling water, using a stick or wooden spoon to push the paper to the bottom. Once all the balls of paper had been immersed in the boiling water, he would cover the pot and reduce the heat, letting the water cool until he could compress the sodden mass of paper by hand. Mr. Koyama experimented by adding seaweed and even powdered soap as well as white clay to the newsprint to achieve a substance as malleable as *keto* itself.

Mr. Reisen Takahata also experimented with the use of boiled newspaper and created a number of extremely beautiful bonkei. It is his belief that newsprint, which does not crack after it has been finally treated, produces results that are more beautiful and more natural than *keto* itself.

My own school follows the Koyama method in its initial stages, bringing about fifty sheets of newspaper to the boil and letting them cool. Then we add about half a pound each of white clay and charcoal, kneading the mixture well. The result is a substance with much the same elasticity as *keto*; furthermore, it can be handled with a spatula in the same way and has the same affinity for white clay in the early modelling stages. It differs from *keto* in that oil paints are more suitable than watery solutions—in large part because the colors of the former do not fade. For the same reason, in the making of this type of dry bonkei, we avoid the use of living trees. We prefer artificial trees that can be bought in shops or that we make ourselves; when we use flowers, they are paper ones. So far as ornaments go, we use the same ones in a dry bonkei that we would use in a bonkei based on *keto*.

Any strong adhesive may be used to ensure that the ornaments stay in place when a framed bonkei is hung on the wall. One thing to bear in mind when making this kind of bonkei is that you must wait for the papier-mâché to dry out completely before you apply any paint to it. The length of time this process takes must depend, naturally, on the materials used as well as on the humidity of the room in which you have put it to dry.

The chief disadvantage of dry bonkei is that it never has the fresh look of one made of *keto*. You must attempt to compensate for this lack by making your oil colors look as fresh as possible; spraying the bonkei with water from time to time will also contribute to a fresh appearance.

TABLE BONKEI

Table bonkei, as I noted earlier, is almost always ceremonial in nature: it may serve as a centerpiece for a dinner party, or it may celebrate some special occasion, such as a wedding ceremony. Although typically Japanese in style, it has gained great popularity in the West. The important point to remember is that it will be viewed from all sides; it must, therefore, be as decorative as possible. The more flowers and trees you use, the happier the result.

Chapter 8 TREES NATURAL AND ARTIFICIAL

As we have noted, the bonkei artist has a wide variety of trees to choose from when the time comes for him to add them to his creation. Usually, in the examples given in this book, we have used a combination of both large, natural trees in the foreground and small, artificial trees in the far distance. The latter may be formed from any number of substances, while for the former I have already referred the reader to *The Masters' Book of Bonsai* (Tokyo, 1967), which gives accurate and complete information beyond the scope of this book.

Nevertheless, since our school uses chiefly living plants and trees (save, of course, in the making of a dry bonkei), I should like to give a brief outline here of our experience in the uses of bonsai trees. *Bon*, as we know, is the Japanese word for tray, and the complete word means merely "planted in a tray": it thus offers little or no problem to the city dweller with limited space; his tray will hold a number of trees which he may choose from when the moment comes for him to transfer a bonsai tree to a bonkei. In addition, if the tree is planted in a rich substance like *keto*

and is watered regularly, it will easily survive the transplantation, and when the bonkei is dismantled, it may be replanted in a bonsai to be used again and again. It is not at all unusual for such a tree to outlast its owner's lifetime.

Bonsai has been known in Japan at least since the time of the famous scrolls of the priest Hōnen (1133–1212), but it is very probable that the art itself is older still and that peasants and farmers used to bring trees and plants home, plant them in special pots, and tend them carefully to keep them small. Bonsai may well be Japan's first practical experience in miniaturization. Later, during the Muromachi period, cherry and pine trees received special attention and were frequently mentioned in literary works of the period.

The word itself, *bonsai*, first appears during the latter part of the Tokugawa period, when the art was specially popular with poets and painters. The latter, however, were mainly attracted by oddly shaped trees, and this fad for deformation persisted until the Meiji Restoration, when bonsai cultivators realized that a well-shaped, healthy, natural tree was preferable to a sickly and ill-shaped one. The first large-scale bonsai exhibition was held in Hibiya Park in 1914, and twenty years later the Tokyo Metropolitan Art Museum began a series of annual exhibitions, which are still held. Bonsai, then, whatever you choose to call it—art, hobby, or mere gardening—is well established in Japan, thus facilitating the task of the bonkei-maker. Any Westerner, however, who desires to grow his own bonsai trees will find that it is not a very difficult hobby to master if he follows a few simple rules. As I said before, I recommend the use of *The Masters Book of Bonsai* or some similar work; here I shall attempt only to outline a little of my own experience in working with these small and fascinating objects.

GENERAL RULES

The chief points to remember are that the bonsai tree must not only be small enough to harmonize with your bonkei but must also have a transcendent beauty that the large tree growing wild in nature sometimes lacks. Do not forget that your tree may live to the age of fifty or more, and that, as it grows older, it takes on a more distinctive and personal character. Your task, then, is not only to keep it small and to trim it so as to bring out its essential beauty but also to allow it to express its age and personality.

To accomplish this three-fold aim you must bear in mind certain essential points:

1. Frequently repot it (the size and shape of the pot are important), give it fresh soil whenever necessary, and trim the roots so that the tree does not receive an excess of nourishment that will cause it to shoot up to an unmanageable height.

2. Both watering and fertilizing must be carefully controlled.

3. The position of the tree (depending, of course, on its species) must be changed according to the season.

4. It must be protected through the regular use of insecticides.

Only experience will teach you when and how to prune and trim the branches to produce precisely the kind of tree you desire, a tree that you may freely display knowing that it will receive the appreciation it deserves.

SOIL

The kind of soil you use is, obviously, of extreme importance. Bonsai experts have tended to favor red loam, as it holds water and has excellent ventilation. The customary method of using red loam is to crush it to a fine powder and then pass it through an extremely fine sieve (with approximately a one-millimeter mesh). Then mix the soil with soft sand, the ratio of soil to sand depending on the species of tree you are hoping to cultivate. Conifers, for example, do best in a mixture that is about forty per cent sand, while the amount is halved for deciduous trees and flowering plants, with about ten per cent of leaf mould added to the mixture.

The purpose of passing the soil through a fine sieve is to

increase its aeration as well as its water-holding ability. The number of times the tree should be watered depends on these two factors, since after the soil is dampened, water takes the place of air in the cells; then, after the water has been absorbed by the action of sun and wind, air replaces the water that has evaporated. This constant alternation of water and air in the soil makes for healthy roots.

With hard soil, even after the water in the air spaces has evaporated, the soil itself contains a certain amount of water which feeds the roots until fresh water is added.

For the purposes of bonsai, we class trees in three groups: those grown from seeds, those grown from cuttings, and those grown from seedlings found in the wild. The beginner will find the last of the three easiest to handle and the first the most difficult, since although the parent tree may be a good one, its seeds seldom inherit those good qualities. The same is not true of cuttings, and seedlings growing wild tend to be sturdy, having survived the perilous first days.

SEEDS

To anyone attempting to grow a bonsai tree from a seed, I would recommend that the moment it exhibits any signs of deformity it be uprooted and discarded. In a field of good soil, such a seed can extend its roots straight down, but in a shallow pot, when the roots grow crooked, so does the burgeoning trunk.

Take, for example, the zelkova. If you want a straight trunk, then you must remove the straight roots from the base of the trunk the moment the new leaves start to appear. This process stunts the growth of the tree and at the same time gives rise to a large number of branches.

SEEDLINGS

The most popular trees for bonsai are: cedar, cypress, pine, orange, spirea, zelkova, cherry, and plum. I recommend that when you go out into the woods looking for suitable seedlings, you have a good look at the parent tree first; it will give you some indication of what possibilities are inherent in the seedling. At the same time, if possible, collect more than one of the same species of seedling; then, when you have taken them home, discard those that do not seem suitable for bonsai. In fields where the grass has been mowed, you will find that the tops of the seedlings have also been lopped off. Their trunks, as a result, are likely to be thick and have interesting shapes.

CUTTINGS

Cuttings taken from evergreens and deciduous trees present slightly different problems. The ideal soil (red loam) is much the same, but it needs enrichment with fertilizers of various kinds and even with vegetable hormones. Cuttings from evergreens, such as the Japanese cedar and the Japanese cypress, are customarily made during the months of March and April, while those from deciduous trees (camellia, fra-

When trimming a tree, use an imaginary triangle to attain a pleasing effect.

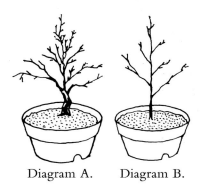

Diagram A.   Diagram B.

The ideal is to make the branches of trees shoot in all directions, as shown in Diagram A; Diagram B illustrates a poor example of trimming.

grant olive, sweet-smelling daphne) are made during the rainy season.

It is not an easy process. Out of ten cuttings planted, the beginner will be lucky if three take root; as he gains increasing experience, the ratio will probably rise to about seven out of ten. The beginner will generally find that he is most fortunate with cedar, cypress, Chinese black pine, and oak; and that he has least luck with fir, hemlock, white birch, hemlock spruce, and beech trees.

TRIMMING

Second only to ensuring firm and vigorous roots is the achievement of an abundance of leaves—a desire the bonkei artist shares with other arboriculturists. And as everyone knows who works with trees, one of the ways of enforcing luxuriant leafage is by means of trimming. Some experts go so far as to trim away all the leaves and wait for the second

growth; this is only practicable, however, if one is sure that the roots are sturdy and healthy. The beginner is advised, therefore, not to do too much trimming at first, but always to leave enough leaves on the tree to prevent it looking bare.

Here are a few points to bear in mind:

1. Excluding plants that hug the ground, the growth points lie in the tips of the branches. Lower branches should not be trimmed to the same degree as upper branches, which grow again and make the whole tree more vigorous; lower branches, if overtrimmed, may simply wither and die. Lower buds lack the vitality of those higher up on the tree.

2. Beginners must resist the temptation to trim the tree so that the branches on either side take on an alternating pattern: this is called "climbing the stairs" in Japan and is not well regarded. The beginner should seek instead to trim the tree so that branches grow in all directions. Trees whose branches (two, three, or even four) grow from one spot are

difficult to handle. When trimming, you must always attempt to make the point where the branch has been removed as inconspicuous as possible. For that reason, trimming should be done as early as is consistent with the growth of the roots. Too much trimming will make the tips of the branches look thick and ugly as opposed to graceful and slender, which is the aim of bonkei.

3. The artist must keep in mind the color of the leaves he wants—whether it be the pale green of spring, the deep green of midsummer, or the red of autumn—and he must take care to ensure balance between the number of leaves on the tree and the size and shape of the tree itself. There are any number of special considerations here; these the artist will discover for himself through experience. The beech, for example, must always be trimmed before the buds grow too large. Other trees (such as the zelkova and maple), whose chief charm is the redness of their leaves, should be trimmed in midsummer, so that the color is at its best in autumn.

4. Never trim an unhealthy tree because the very act of trimming may kill it. Make every attempt to restore it, nourish it, and if necessary trim away the largest leaves so that they will not sap its vitality further.

5. After trimming, give the tree less water than before, since the cutting away of the leaves decreases evaporation, and if you continue to give the tree as much water as you did, you may rot the roots and so kill the tree.

6. The most important period in the life of a tree is spring, when trees undergo their major growth period. It is then that you must attempt to keep the buds from burgeoning out if you want to ensure that the leaves turn red in autumn.

7. Autumn is the season when you should never do any trimming; once that season is past, you may trim both leaves and branches so as to achieve the most desirable form. (All the precepts I have listed above have been passed down from generation to generation in Japan for many centuries. I may say that I observe them religiously in creating my own bonsai trees and have never regretted doing so.)

WATERING
A few more suggestions familiar to anyone who has grown trees (whether bonsai or not) may be helpful to the beginner. For one thing, a young tree can absorb only limited amounts of water and direct sunlight. Either, in excess, may kill it—so it should be exposed only gradually to strong sunshine, and the amount of water that it is given at first should be carefully rationed. In fact, it should be given no more water than is necessary to keep it alive. The most frequent cause of death among young trees is excessive watering.

FERTILIZING
On the question of fertilizing, we in Japan prefer oil-meal cake to chemicals. The amount and time of fertilizing must vary, naturally, with the climate; in Japan, we adhere

roughly to the following schedule (which may be indicative, if not definitive, to the Westerner): after the buds appear in springtime, we fertilize the tree two or three times a month until the beginning of the rainy season in late June; then we refrain from fertilizing during the wet midsummer months, and resume the twice- or thrice-monthly fertilizing in autumn, not only to help the tree withstand the winter cold, but also to encourage the growth of healthy buds the following spring. The fertilizer we use, by the way, is always dissolved in water.

To help the tree overcome the onslaughts of such destructive insects as aphides and the May beetle, we use insecticides like nicotine, BHC, or DDT.

PLANTING IN KETO

As I have noted, my school of bonkei prefers live trees, so their cultivation is one of our chief occupations and joys. We feel that living plants and trees greatly enhance a *keto* bonkei and make it seem to glow with vitality, which is one of the chief advantages of *keto* as against such "dead" materials as papier-mâché or plaster of paris. My school also tends to prefer small-leaved trees.

Our method is to wrap the roots of the tree in newspaper after depotting it; we then soak them in water, and plant them in the *keto*. This method, we believe, helps to preserve water around the roots of the tree and so keep it alive; at the same time, when we dismantle the bonkei, the tree may be removed from the *keto* without damage to the roots due to the protective coating of paper. If you have been assiduous in the watering of your bonkei, the tree will thrive and so may be repotted and used again innumerable times.

On occasion you will find it more expedient to take a small sprig from a large tree and make it play the role of a whole tree in your bonkei. In that case, you will naturally want to select branches with plentiful foliage. These you press directly into the *keto*.

Always wrap the roots of your bonsai trees in wet newspaper before planting them in *keto*.

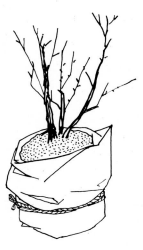

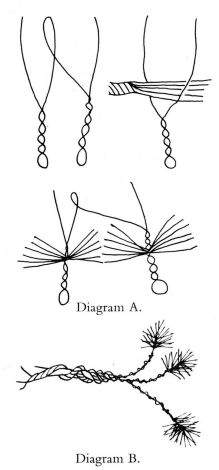

Diagram A.

Diagram B.

These diagrams show how to make the branches of a pine tree, using twisted wire and hemp fibers.

ARTIFICIAL TREES

As we have noted, however, it is not always possible or even desirable to use exclusively live trees in our bonkei; so there arises the question of how best to make artificial trees serve our purpose. Here again experience is the best teacher, and, with practice, you will soon hit upon the materials most suitable for the various kinds of trees you wish to use.

Here, I shall give my method for making only one kind of artificial tree—the pine—but similar procedures may be adapted for many other species. The materials I use are manila hemp, wire, artificial moss, dyeing and coloring powders, and cement or varnish. I first make the trunk of the tree by twisting a number of strands of very slender wire together; these same wires, once the trunk is formed, may be spread out to form the branches of the tree. Thus I am free to make them take any shape I desire.

Now I untwist a hempen clothes line and fray the edges; then, to straighten the fibers so that they take on the appearance of pine needles, I dye them in a green solution and afterwards leave five or six strands wrapped in paper for a time.

Using the same kind of wire as that which I made the trunk of the tree and its branches out of, I cut off a number of three-inch lengths. As shown in Diagram A (at left), I bend each wire and twist it briefly before inserting the hemp, and then twist it again so that the hemp is held firmly. I trim the ends of the pine needles, then cut away the twisted wire (*diagram B*), leaving only enough space to attach a pine cone. Three such rows of hemp may be combined to form a branch.

Having your framework—trunk, branches, and needles—you now must solve the problem of making the whole acquire the patina of age. (In Japan, pine trees are always considered, particularly in a bonkei landscape, as trees that live long.) If you take the obvious course of painting the trunk with Chinese white and then with poster color, you will fail to give this necessary impression of age. A far better method is to paint the trunk with cement or glue, and then scatter artificial brownish moss over it. (Incidentally, sawdust may be substituted for the moss if it is first passed through a fine sieve and then dyed an appropriate color.)

Once the cement and moss have dried, paint the trunk with varnish and scatter green moss over it. The result makes the trunk of a tree seem so ancient that it appears to have accumulated a heavy coat of moss. Should you desire to make a large pine, do not twist wires together to form the trunk, but rather take the dried branches of a tree and wire them together, or, if you happen to find a shape that pleases you, use branches alone.

In the making of an artificial tree, it is always important to study a living tree first, its shape, the arrangement of its branches, and its geographical position. For example, pine trees growing by the sea, in the mountains, or on sandy ground are all noticeably different. The same is true of the colors of the trunks of various trees; you must then make sure that the moss you buy, or the sawdust you dye, is of the correct color. It goes without saying that an artificial tree should resemble to as great an extent as possible its living counterpart.

GLOSSARY OF MATERIALS AND SUBSTITUTES

BENIGARA: Colcothar, a reddish brown pigment, which is mixed with water. If unavailable, substitute a powdered dye of the same color, or poster color.

HAKUDO: A grayish white powder mixed with water. Any powdered whitish clay, as sold by ceramic supply stores for example, can be substituted.

ISOSUNA: A general title for three types of sand—*chūiso*, *koiso*, and *ōiso*. All are grayish brown in color and rough in texture. Of the three, *ōiso* has the largest grains, *koiso* the finest. *Chūiso* is usually used for shores, *koiso* for shallow water, and *ōiso* for more distant water.

KETO: Peat, preferably composed of the humus of marsh reeds. A good substitute is papier-mâché, a mixture of boiled newspaper and sifted clay.

MAKI-GOKE: Artificial moss. If an adequate substitute cannot be found in toy shops or elsewhere, use fine sawdust, dyeing it according to the shade desired. Dyed strands of hemp, cut into small pieces, are another alternative.

MAZUNA: A very fine gray sand used only for rivers and lakes.

MICHISUNA: A brown, large-grained sand used for roads, etc.

NAMISUNA: Powdered calcite or marble used to represent rough water. A substitute is fine white sand.

POWDERED GYPSUM: Used to represent snow on distant mountains. An alternative is lime or chalk.

SPATULA: A metal implement with narrow handle and flat, thin, flexible face. A round-ended palette knife of suitable size could be used in bonkei. The kind of knife used for icing cakes might be effective in large-scale work.

TONOKO: A yellowish brown dye mixed with a little clay and water. A substitute is poster color. If this fades, further coats should be added.

VERDIGRIS: A green pigment to which either a blue powder or yellow lead and purple dye are added. Poster color or a dye of the same color are alternatives.